Something's Wrong.
Let's Fix It.

Something's Wrong. Let's Fix It.

A Personal Political Memoir

SUSAN P. SCHAFER, Ed.D.

Something's Wrong. Let's Fix It. A Personal Political Memoir © Copyright 2024 Susan P. Schafer, Ed.D.

All rights reserved. No part of this publication may be reproduced, distributed, or transmitted in any form or by any means, including photocopying, recording, or other electronic or mechanical methods, without the prior written permission of the publisher, except in the case of brief quotations embodied in critical reviews and certain other noncommercial uses permitted by copyright law.

Although the author and publisher have made every effort to ensure that the information in this book was correct at press time, the author and publisher do not assume and hereby disclaim any liability to any party for any loss, damage, or disruption caused by errors or omissions, whether such errors or omissions result from negligence, accident, or any other cause.

Adherence to all applicable laws and regulations, including international, federal, state, and local governing professional licensing, business practices, advertising, and all other aspects of doing business in the US, Canada, or any other jurisdiction is the sole responsibility of the reader and consumer.

Scripture quotations are taken from the New Revised Standard Version Updated Edition. Copyright © 2021 National Council of Churches of Christ in the United States of America. Used by permission. All rights reserved worldwide.

This book is a memoir. It reflects the author's present recollections of experiences over time. Some names and characteristics have been changed, some events have been compressed, and some dialogue has been recreated.

ISBN: 979-8-89316-243-1 - paperback
ISBN: 979-8-89316-242-4 - ebook

DEDICATION

Mary S. Mahrer
Nathan A. Mahrer
Ilsa O. Mahrer
Ann S. Meiggs
Michael T. Meiggs
Audrey L. Meiggs
Ava G. Meiggs
Barbara L. Nash
Mary Tate-Phillips
Edwin Gillilan Pierce and Mary Pauline Hosack Haskell Pierce
Susan Tate Pyle
Sakiko Rose Pyle

Table of Contents

Dedication		v
Chapter 1:	Early Life and Loss	1
Chapter 2:	Rebounding from War to Enrichment	15
Chapter 3:	Teenage Tensions and Grief	25
Chapter 4:	Moving to the Wild West	41
Chapter 5:	Higher Education and New Teacher's Blunders	53
Chapter 6:	An Ugly Yet Hopeful World	69
Chapter 7:	Marriage, Motherhood, and Sexism	75
Chapter 8:	Graduate School and Growing an Activist Backbone	85
Chapter 9:	Troubled Waters	97
Chapter 10:	Mission Accomplished with Title IX	107
Chapter 11:	Leadership Training for Girls and Women	121
Chapter 12:	Seeking the Gay Goddess	135
Chapter 13:	Modern Family Lives	147
Chapter 14:	From Horror to Joy	153
Chapter 15:	From Education Careers to New Adventures	161
Chapter 16:	More Aspirations	169
Chapter 17:	It's Not a Job. It's a Calling	177
Chapter 18:	Novice Legislator and World Traveler	187
Chapter 19:	Fixing What's Wrong	199
Chapter 20:	It Appears Perfect	215

Chapter 21:	The Four-Year Nightmare	227
Chapter 22:	Finding Joy During the Four-Year Nightmare 2016–2020	233
Chapter 23:	From Sunrise to Sunset	241
Appendices		247
Acknowledgments		257

I have walked many miles and tried not to falter. I've made mistakes along the way. I've discovered after fixing something there are many more problems to fix but not by myself.

Nelson B. Mandela

CHAPTER 1

Early Life and Loss

Standing and trembling one morning in my high school principal's office at the age of fifteen, I decided to speak truth to power. Things were very wrong at my high school, and I was determined to fix them. As an obedient, skinny kid from a modest duplex in Lincoln, Nebraska, I was mad that during the summer tennis leagues I could defeat over half of the boys on the Lincoln High School (LHS) tennis team, but when the fall season came I was banned from competing. I was told that the regular fall season tennis was for boys only. My tall blond summer tennis coach, Mr. Colson, agreed with me and advised me to speak with the principal, Mr. Bogar, who carried a bullhorn in the halls directing kids to quiet down and behave. Somehow, mustering up what little courage I did have, I made an appointment with his secretary who looked at me suspiciously. One week later, I tiptoed into Mr. Bogar's oak-paneled office, slowly peering around with my hands shaking and sweat rolling down my face.

I implored, "Please, Mr. Bogar, I can defeat half of our boys in the summer tennis league. So why can't I play in the fall season team with them or have a girls' team?"

Fiddling with his #2 yellow pencil, mustache twitching, Mr. Bogar, a stout former football coach who resembled Rough Rider Teddy Roosevelt explained, "Look, honey, the tennis team is for boys only. There isn't any money for girls' sports or girls' coaches. No money for girls' uniforms, equipment or locker rooms, no girls interested, and no other girls' teams our girls could compete against. And the Nebraska High School Athletic Association doesn't sanction girls' sports because females are too weak to play competitively. Listen, playing sports could cause your uterus to fall out. But go talk to Miss Weatherspoon. She might be sympathetic." I wasn't even certain what a uterus was.

Furious, but smiling politely, I backed out of his office and silently declared, "Something's wrong! Let's fix it. There ought to be a law to require sports for girls, and we all will somehow make it happen." And then, having just read *Macbeth* in literature class, I channeled Lady Macbeth. "I shall screw my courage to a sticking place, and I will not fail."

But advocating with assistant principal Miss Weatherspoon, a bespectacled, ninety-pound, sixty-year-old school marm who resembled a nun in her orthopedic shoes, flowing black skirt, and a floppy dark brown sweater, was mission impossible. She barely looked up at me from her black rotary dial phone and stacks of legal pads and wearily said, "Don't you know that students shouldn't complain about school rules?" Later she telephoned my mother, Polly Hosack Haskell Pierce, telling her that I had "confronted" Mr. Bogar. My mother prophetically told me I did well to speak up when something is wrong, to speak truth to power, and that she was proud of me!

Okay, something is wrong, like sexism in sports. What else? Do I have the courage to fix other wrongs? Are other people willing to help? If so, how? When? What will changes cost? Why do we fix these wrongs? I was becoming a social reformer and activist at age fifteen. But where did my determination and courage come from at such a young age?

I was born a World War Two (WWII) and Franklin D. Roosevelt (FDR) war baby in Portland, Maine. Later my family and I moved to Lincoln, Nebraska. Some historical developments of that era included the invention of an "exciting" new item of apparel called the T-shirt, Humphrey Bogart and Ingrid Bergman becoming lovers in *Casablanca,* and Nazi Germany building crematoriums to exterminate six million Jewish men, women, and children.

My parents were middle class and very hardworking. We were blessed to spend years in Maine where waves crash on rocky shores and white-washed lighthouses beam of dangers ahead. My parents set out to help me achieve my highest potential, which the gospel of the American Dream promised to us white children. Maine is rugged and strong, so chances were good for me, right? Most importantly, however, I acknowledge how my parents' difficult lives influenced my determination to overcome many personal, professional, and political obstacles. Thankfully, I am the product of four strong cultures: the precipitous New England coast, which taught me to be daring and courageous; the wild Nebraska prairie, which taught me to confront challenges with determination and grit; the abundant Pennsylvania farmland, teaching me to be generous with any bounty I have; and later the rugged Rocky Mountains, which taught me to strive and climb higher in nature and in life.

I am the offspring of several courageous great-grandparents, grandparents, and parents who gave me strong roots and wings. I will tell their stories of courage and perseverance, which motivated me to emulate them. I hope to be as fine a parent and grandparent as they were to me and my sister. My father, Lt. Colonel Edwin G. Pierce

(1902–1974), was one of five children and was born at home in rural Orleans, Nebraska, on the windswept western prairie. My paternal grandparents, Wendell Phillips Pierce (1867–1916) and Elizabeth Coleman Gillilan Pierce (1867–1953), had migrated to Nebraska from Ohio. Grandfather Wendell, a slender, tall, dark, and handsome businessman, was president of the Orleans National Bank, a realtor, and a church deacon. Grandmother Elizabeth, a tall, strong, stout brunette, tended vegetable gardens and apple orchards, raised five children without indoor plumbing or electricity, delivered babies, and volunteered fifty years as an activist in the Methodist Church and the Order of the Eastern Star. For fun, their children rode horses, played hide and seek in the fields, and jumped in haystacks. For work, they helped with the vegetable gardens and crops of wheat and corn while getting educated in the chilly, windblown one-room schoolhouse.

My father was the youngest son among siblings Walker, Joseph, Dorothy, and Mary. My dad's two bossy older sisters told him that he *must* attend the University of Nebraska (NU) for business so that when their father retired, he could manage the family bank. "Eddie, if you learn the banking business, you'll be a success for life!" They intended to earn teaching certificates, but teaching wasn't easy back then in those barren one-room schoolhouses. Teachers had to haul in wood, light the fire, teach thirty kids of all ages and abilities, and bring sack lunches for those who had nothing but hot barley water to eat at breakfast. Life was difficult but going well for the Pierces.

But unexpectedly, tragedy struck. A runaway team of horses killed Grandfather Wendell while he was out on an evening walk. Was he trying to subdue the team or protect other people near the upheaval? Probably. His untimely death at the age of forty-nine left the leadership of the bank to my college freshman father, and the upbringing of five children to my now widowed Grandmother Elizabeth.

My father spent a few years managing the bank as best he could, but then even more tragedy struck. The 1929 stock market crash destroyed small and large banks and left Dad struggling to find any kind of job anywhere. Then one day at the local general store, he saw a dusty Esso Oil calendar with a green and blue photograph of Moosehead Lake in the Longfellow Mountains in faraway Maine. Dad mused, "I'll take the Union Pacific to search for a job in Maine and do some fishing and hiking."

Good luck greeted him upon his arrival. The Fidelity Bank of Portland was advertising for a cashier, and Dad was hired. However, with dark storm clouds blowing in from Europe and a psychopath named Adolph Hitler leading the German Nazi party, American men were warned they might lose their jobs if drafted to go fight with the Allies. Women would replace the men as machinists, welders, accountants, cashiers, and riveters. "I still need to find a good steady job and a beautiful woman for a wife," dreamed Dad. But Germany was rearming after its loss in WWI, and military service might be in Dad's future. Germany was not accepting its WWI defeat, which sadly meant more possible deaths of American service members in another war. My father, like his father, was tall, dark, and handsome with an outgoing, charismatic personality; even years later at socials with my friends, my dad would charm them all. And I aspired to be like him in several respects—friendly, smiling, and engaging with everyone. A lesson learned from my father in his early years: life presents accidents and challenges, so we seek opportunities, we grasp courage, we keep our hands on the plow, and we keep forging ahead.

Meanwhile my mother, Mary Pauline (Polly) Hosack Haskell Pierce (1903–1992), was one of seven children born to Mary Etta Daugherty Hosack (Irish) and Edwin Richard Hosack (Scots) in Mercer, Pennsylvania, forty miles northwest of Pittsburgh. Her siblings were Harry, Kathryn, Robert, Mabel, Richard, and Dorothy. Polly was five foot five with wavy brown hair, very energetic, with sparkly blue eyes and an infectious laugh. These Hosacks were descendants of pioneer families who were deeded eighty acres of Pennsylvania land for the Hosack officers' service and heroism in the 1776 Revolutionary War. In 1895 my great-grandparents planted forty-two willow and maple trees that still stand today, forming a breezy green canopy over a brook that flows along the farmhouse.

Before her marriage, my grandmother Mary attended Grove City College and became a teacher, excelling in the art of elocution (public speaking). She was strong and stout, with salt-and-pepper hair in a bun and always an apron over her snow-white dress. She tended apple and cherry orchards while raising pigs, chickens, and seven rambunctious children. Daily she cooked, baked, and did laundry often with a nursing baby at her breast; she and other pioneer women were accomplished multitaskers! I'm sure she often was also called to help deliver babies. Could we women today do all of that? I doubt it.

When swarming locusts, blizzards, and droughts destroyed their crops, Grandmother's attitude was "We will forget and thankfully move on." Lesson learned for me. She even served as an activist committee woman for the Mercer County Republican Party, fighting for safety nets for small business owners and strongly working for the 19th Amendment to the US Constitution that was passed in 1920 and guaranteed women the right to vote. Seventy years later, I somehow channeled Grandmother Mary and campaigned to become a Democratic State Representative in the Colorado House of Representatives. I apparently inherited a passion for social justice from this female role model. One of my greatest regrets in life is never getting to meet this inspiring farmer who died young at age seventy-one.

Meanwhile my maternal grandfather, Edwin R. Hosack, was a wheat and oats farmer, town sheriff, and commercial dairyman who delivered milk by horse and cart to coal miners' families who barely spoke any English. He was five foot ten, wore denim bib overalls, sported a silver mustache, and always had a smile on his face. He also raised cattle and pigs, so ham, sausage, and liverwurst were the family's protein staples. But he loved his cows, sheep, and pigs so much that he couldn't slaughter them and had to hire a butcher to do that for him. He always bowed his head and said grace before dinner. One appetite I inherited from him was a sweet tooth. After every supper, he'd ask, "Where are the cake or the cookies?" My words exactly.

He was able to provide for his family with a farmhouse but not with any indoor heating, plumbing, or electricity. However, the Hosack farmhouse was the first in Mercer County to have the "luxury" of a party-line telephone in 1930, but subscribers were limited to ten minutes of talking so the other party could have their ten minutes.

Mom recalls sleeping on a sagging straw mattress with three restless sisters in the drafty upstairs bedroom while her three brothers slept with their parents on the ground floor room with freezing gales blustering through. Mom mastered the rugged farm life but not those frigid night trips to the outhouse. She worked long hours chopping wood, doing laundry, and cooking but found fun in feeding cows and chickens, collecting eggs, and riding in her dad's wagon to deliver milk to low-income Italian families. I inherited grit and strength from her.

On the other hand, Kate, Mom's sophisticated oldest sister, hated farm life even though she took care of her younger siblings and sewed dresses for them. Kate bolted from the farm upon high school graduation and moved to Grove City, Pennsylvania, where she wrote book reviews and later married a prominent University of Pittsburgh professor, George Gould, PhD. Kate was five foot ten with a high beehive of gold hair. She wore flowing black dresses and was adorned with gold earrings and bracelets. Since there were no high schools near the Hosack family farm, Kate decided to board little sister Polly in Grove City to teach her proper etiquette and charm for later interacting with what Kate thought would be Pittsburgh high society. Kate stated, "Farm life is a bit bourgeois and beneath one's dignity. Reach for the best! Don't settle for milking cows, feeding pigs, and cleaning out barns. You can become a proper lady." Mom was perplexed but always obeyed Kate's commands.

Kate was also a teacher of writing in Grove City and later in Pittsburgh, thus the art of writing thankfully runs in my family. Kate even published her first book at age five and later in life organized the Pittsburg Literary Group, which encouraged reading and discussing classics such as *For Whom the Bells Tolls, A Tree Grows in Brooklyn,* and *The Diary of Anne Frank.* The group also taught free writing classes to citizens and immigrants who wanted to learn more than what was taught in junior and senior high schools.

Kate's four years of "charm school" taught Mom how to set formal dinnerware, how to address authority, and how to wear the latest 1930s fashions, even though the shoes were so tight they left bunions on her feet for the rest of her life. She gained the expertise needed to polish sterling pitchers, select the finest Wedgwood china, carve a roast beef, set perfect place settings, make proper introductions, and attract the opposite sex with coy smiles and flirtatious conversation. Kate had mastered Professor Henry Higgins's dictate in George Bernard Shaw's 1913 play *Pygmalion* to "always show proper breeding," and Mom became like social striver, Eliza Doolittle. The play later became the best seller *My Fair Lady.* The lessons I learned from Aunt Kate and Mom: etiquette, manners, and courtesy served me extremely well in my life.

So it was that Mom, clumsily practicing sister Kate's "high society skills" met a handsome young, osteopathy intern while she was working as a secretary at an automobile dealership. Dr. Albert Haskell, a tall, six-foot-one blond gentleman was shopping for a car. They blinked, smiled shyly, and flirted a bit with each other, thinking they'd never see each other again. But fate intervened when Mom underwent a tonsillectomy. "I can't believe how lucky I am! My attending doctor is that Albert Haskell and he is gorgeous," screamed Mom to her sisters. Done. Mom and Albert courted for six months in Grove City, then in Philadelphia, and later married in Pittsburgh in 1928, all set for a joyful life ahead.

Albert completed residencies in Maine and Massachusetts while Mom won an administrative job at the private Bates College in Lewiston, Maine. "Let's go hear the Boston Pops and that great conductor, Arthur Fiedler," dreamed Mom. "I want romantic picnics at the Maine Pemaquid Point Lighthouse," dreamed Albert. With Albert finally earning that marathon osteopathy degree, Dr. and Mrs. Albert Haskell were living large; nothing could go wrong, could it?

Throughout this book, I tell some sad family stories that still influence my beliefs, values, and decisions. Could I recover when things would go wrong in my life when they inevitably did? And things did go terribly wrong for the young Haskell couple. First, Albert reluctantly admitted he'd made the wrong decision to become an osteopath, and he decided to apply to Tufts University Medical School in Boston to earn an MD after four long and costly years in osteopathy college. Mom found jobs with the Boston Girl Scouts and financed Al's four years of medical school. Upon his graduation from Tufts, Albert told Mom that he had a hernia problem and wanted the surgery done before he set up his medical practice. "Hernia surgeries are a bit risky, but I have the best urologist in Boston," Albert reassured

Mom. What could possibly go wrong? Albert's hernia operation had deadly results. The love of Mom's life, the young Dr. Albert Haskell, died a week later at age thirty-three, leaving heartbreak and despair for his family and for my future mother.

Distraught and in severe grief, what could a young widow do? She and Al had planned to buy a home in Maine and start a family. "Just move on" advised her parents, sisters, friends, and ministers. But Mom cried, "Why did this happen to me? Where was God?" She was so depressed she felt that ending her life was her only option. Thankfully, she could rely on Albert's family, the Hobsons, to help her cope with her grief and to make burial arrangements. Mom buried him in the Hobson plot at the Portland, Maine, Evergreen Cemetery. The Hobsons were Albert's uncle and aunt, and their daughter, Alberta, was Al's only cousin. So, Alberta and her mother, my Aunt Kit, became a sisterly force for good in Mom's struggling recovery, and Mom later returned to her Girl Scouts job in Boston. Even after sixty years Mom wrote in her 1970 memoir, "Al's loss is still so painful I cannot write one word about it."

After three years of grieving, worthless prayers and counseling, a tiny sliver of hope emerged from a fellow Girl Scouts secretary. A Christian Scientist, Claire, invited Mom to visit the Mother Church of the First Church of Christ Scientist in Boston. "Hey, Polly, why don't you come with me Wednesday night to hear testimonies about emotional and physical healings," coaxed Claire. Mom was nervous and dubious about this outing and didn't even know Claire that well. But when Mom heard stories of healings from persons who had recovered from cancer, heart disease, alcoholism, depression, and a child's suicide, she thought these "healings" were just luck, magical thinking, not actual healings. Mom thanked Claire and said she'd go one more time and wanted desperately to believe the gold inscriptions in the sanctuary: Divine love always has met and always will meet every human need. Mom wondered, *Could this statement be true? Could this Christian Science help me? I certainly have a human need.* And Mom continued attending the Wednesday and Sunday services with Claire and began studying the history of the Christian Science Church.

Mary Baker Eddy, the founder of Christian Science was raised in the Congregational Church and wrote interpretations from the Bible into her book, *Science and Health with Key to the Scriptures.* But Mom did question if this Mary Baker Eddy was one of those faith healers like Pentecostal Sister Aimee McPherson or fictional Evangelist Sister Sharon in *Elmer Gantry.* But no, Mrs. Eddy was not an Evangelist shouting at desperate worshippers in drab olive canvas tents. She was an author and religious leader who explained Jesus's teachings and healings from the first century and applied them to the twentieth century.

During this grieving period, Mom slowly did gain hope by studying *Science and Health with Key to the Scriptures.* She sat transfixed every Wednesday night with Claire hearing true stories of healings, reading the international *Christian Science Monitor* newspaper (now a magazine) and never missing a Sunday morning service complete with Bible readings, lessons from *Science and Health,* and Mrs. Eddy's hymns like "Shepherd, Show Me How to Go." A few lyrics:

> Shepherd, show me how to go, over the hillside steep.
> How to gather, how to sow, how to feed thy sheep.
> I will listen for Thy voice, lest my footsteps stray.
> I will follow and rejoice all the rugged way.

It is often said that Christian Scientists don't believe in doctors. I personally believe in the power of God, the power in Christian Science, and in western medicine. My mother often said that Christian

Science (CS) also stands for Common Sense. For example, when she heard about polio vaccinations for children, she was the first to get my sister and me in line. When neither western medicine nor anything else helps, many people are desperate and turn to Christian Science. Today on Wednesday nights in every Christian Science church at seven o'clock, attendees speak about their physical and mental healings by praying to God and believing in God's power to heal.

My mother, Polly, slowly prayed and took hold of God and Christian Science, and after four years her grief had subsided. She reluctantly agreed to a blind date with a so-called "handsome bachelor," Ed Pierce from Nebraska who worked as a banker in Portland, Maine. Ed had friends in Boston who knew Mom, and they arranged a dinner date, and this attractive gentleman showed some promise. But this eastern girl had to study a map to locate Nebraska, which she thought was a "hick" state. Surprise! Ed actually was handsome and charismatic, and Nebraska was a beautiful and bountiful state after all. Several sparks flew. After many dates, expensive long-distance phone calls, and Penn Central rides between Boston and Portland, Mom and Dad decided to marry in 1941 at the Congregational Church in Lexington, Massachusetts.

Blessedly thankful to God and Christian Science, Mom recovered to restart her next life on the Maine coast with her second husband, Edwin Gillilan Pierce. She planned to enjoy a loving and stable life as a banker's wife and, God willing, a mother. Lessons I learned from Mom's turbulent life are the power of God, the Bible, prayer, hymns, generosity, and courage that have thankfully guided my entire life.

Fortunately, my mother's Christian Science spirituality was compatible with my father's Protestant Congregational Church's teachings, which my sister and I also studied. So I was blessed to grow up in two strong communities of faith. I am proud of the historic, liberal Congregational Church United Church of Christ (UCC) in the United States that stood early for the abolition of slavery; the right of women to vote and to be ordained as ministers; for social justice, civil rights, and the ban on nuclear weapons. This church also believes that no matter who you are or where you are on life's journey, you are welcome there. The Congregational Church is open and affirming, meaning that lesbians, gays, bisexuals, trans, and queer persons are welcome in its community of believers. Thus what feeds my soul is both the Christian Science Church with its belief in the power of God, the Bible, and Mrs. Eddy's writings, and the Congregational Church with its powerful sermons, hymns, choirs, Bible studies, and charitable outreach. I am blessed and thankful for them both that have inspired and guided me my entire life.

CHAPTER 2

Rebounding from War to Enrichment

Fear and terror struck my mother again. The German Nazi dictator Adolph Hitler invaded America's allies on the European continent. Might Mom's new husband possibly be drafted into the Army? "Not fair! Wars are dangerous! How can this happen to me after I've just lost Albert," cried Mom. But for Ed, the American red, white, and blue draft in 1941 to go fight the "Nazis and Japs," as he called them, promised an adventurous opportunity for him to prove himself and to help "ensure the blessings of liberty" for his country. Travel to jolly old England and la belle France, become a military officer, protect your country, and prove your manhood! Intoxicated with visions of heroism in war, Dad volunteered in the first draft and passed the IQ test to earn a second lieutenant commission in the US Army Air Corps. "What a thrill!" he proclaimed.

However, Dad's first assignment was not to a glamorous haute couture capital of Europe but to Los Alamos, New Mexico, near Santa Fe for some secret Manhattan project with a scientist named Oppenheimer. And before moving to New Mexico, I was born in Portland, Maine, on August 2 at Maine Medical as Dad's first daughter.

Back then it was customary for parents to write a note to their newborn and my mother wrote this to me: *Thank you, dear God, for sending this beautiful baby girl. May you always be as lovely as you are today.* But giving birth in the 1940s almost killed my mother and other mothers—for example, long deliveries without epidurals and "bed rest" in hospitals for seven days for a mother to regain her strength, but this bed rest often severely weakened or killed her. Compare those dangers to today when two hours after a normal birth the nurse will say, "Stand up, Mom, carry your baby down the hall to have them cleaned, then go back to your room, and start breastfeeding. You'll be discharged in six hours."

Dad and his company thought this Manhattan project run by some Dr. Oppenheimer was just some research, probably nothing to worry about. They did wonder, however, why hundreds of men in suits and ties carrying brief cases packed into a large building with a Top Secret Do Not Enter sign on its façade. Although he was not a scientist, Dad and the other officers who were building air bases eventually learned that this project was actually to develop the first atomic bomb, to be used if necessary in a possible second world war. And Dad did realize it was safe enough to bring his wife, Polly, and me to Los Alamos. Unconvinced at first about moving from Portland, Mom started dreaming of sunny blue skies, mariachi bands, habanero salsas, and hikes among towering saguaros. And she did decide this move could be novel and exciting for an eastern girl.

After officer training school, Dad's unit did build US Army Air Corps bases. One of his assignments was as the commanding officer of an African American company of 450 inexperienced men. Dad was able to raise their efficiency from unsatisfactory to superior in only sixty days, an accomplishment that earned him the rank of captain and his company's future deployment to the European battlegrounds.

In retrospect, I wonder if any Black men could have been promoted as commander? Of course. Certainly, race discrimination allowed white men and women to win promotions back then just as it does to this day.

Using his experience, Dad was ordered to England in 1944 as a base adjutant and ground executive officer of 2,500 men. He drafted top secret and confidential orders for the tactical group of the powerful US Ninth Air Force's plans for France. He prepared his company for its Normandy air bombing raids, and his men later constructed bases on French soil after the Omaha and Utah Beaches had been stormed. My father's company also helped to bomb and thereby force the superior German army farther back east. The Germans had doubted that the Allies would launch their attack on the treacherous cliffs of Normandy, but they were wrong.

Dad was a leader in this Allied invasion known as D-day (June 6, 1944), which was broadcast twenty-four hours daily over scratchy, static radios: "Thousands of Americans are dying every day in France and on the Omaha and Utah Beaches," lamented CBS broadcaster Edward R. Murrow. Dad saw the dismembered bodies of young soldiers, civilians, and burned children; he saw scorched French farms, fields, hedgerows, churches, and homes. Seeing such destruction, Dad despaired that it was such a waste to lose crops, livestock, and forests and how disgusting the Panzer tanks were, even desecrating cemeteries. "Do Germans have no sense of respect?" wondered Dad.

Dad's fantasies of drinking Moët Chandon at the Folies Bergère cabaret and nibbling strawberry tarts along the Champs-Élysées soon were replaced by the horrors of war: earth-shattering explosions thrusting rocks, trees, missiles, and machines into smoky air that he could not breathe. This D-day assault began on June 6, 1944, and lasted three days. Sixteen hundred Americans sacrificed their lives for us. Were the D-day and the Normandy Invasion the turning point of World War II? Military scholars say yes.

I am still so proud of my father who reported to Supreme Allied Commander, General Dwight D. Eisenhower (Ike) and other leaders regarding strategic decisions in the European Theater of Operations. Dad even told me stories of how Eisenhower, in spite of the Army Air Corps' policy that ALCOHOL IN THE FIELD AND ON BASE IS STRICTLY PROHIBITED would host "happy hours" for the *esprit de corps* of officers and pass around complimentary Camel cigarettes and bottles of Jim Beam. Dad said Ike, born in Denison, Texas, and a graduate of the US Military Academy at West Point, was a "regular guy." Neither superior or conceited, he often chatted socially with his men to make them feel needed and important. Months later Ike did grant Dad leave to finally visit sights and sounds of London and Paris. How this was arranged I do not know.

Years later after Dad had returned from the war as a veteran, he told me to travel the world, especially to Paris, and to learn French, which I did. He taught me basic French words and told me about the spectacles of the Eiffel Tower, the Champs-Élysées, and the Arc de Triomphe. He blushed when speaking of the Folies Bergère filled with alcohol-infused international soldiers who hadn't seen a woman in over a year. But he rarely spoke of the carnage, blood, suffering, and deaths of millions of soldiers, innocent civilians, animals, and children. Trying to spare me the horrors of war, he most often spoke of the bravery, valor, and sacrifices of the men and women with whom he served. I believe we war babies have a duty and responsibility to pass down to our children and grandchildren their grandparents' sacrifices and heroism. With only 119,550 American WWII veterans alive today in 2023, it is our solemn duty to tell the stories of this epic era that changed the course of history.

My father had written me this sentiment just a month after I was born: "Susan, you are more than I could hope for. It is your country's strong belief that we are fighting for a just cause in the hope for peace for future generations." How prophetic. I thank my father and the millions of Allied men and women who dedicated and sacrificed their lives so there has been mostly peace on American soil for my generation.

Although fearing a second world war and the results of the Oppenheimer-Manhattan project, my mother did enjoy the cool New Mexico air and the camaraderie with officers and their families. Life on the base for wives and children provided distractions with birthday parties and picnics, even as scratchy radio broadcasts every day brought dreary news of fiery air raids and death camps overseas. Of course, I as Baby Susan loved the Army life and became a tiny social butterfly long before social media went viral. Each time I saw a soldier in khaki trousers, I ran over, hugged his knees, and screamed "Daddy!" The men laughed with joy at having a surrogate toddler to toss up, tickle, and hug. Apparently I circled many soldiers many times enjoying all the attention and notoriety. Yet as pleasant as Los Alamos was for families, however, WWII was killing thousands of Americans, so Mom decided that she and I must move to be with family since her husband was overseas. She chose Grove City, Pennsylvania, where her youngest sister, Dorothy, lived. She told Mom, "We sisters need to support each other because we could become widows. Harold was badly injured and barely escaped death in the fiery naval battle of the Philippines."

More complications. Shortly before Dad had deployed to Europe again, Mom was thrilled to learn she was expecting a second baby! What joy! My little sister, Mary Elizabeth, was born on June 11, 1944, in Grove City, Pennsylvania, and was nicknamed the D-Day

Baby, which was close enough to June 6, 1944. Far less joyful was the certainty that our father was in France preparing for continuous German assaults.

Meanwhile, on the Pennsylvania home front, I as a toddler became jealous of the baby sister dominating Mother's attention and once angrily grabbed a swatch of infant Mary's hair. Baby Mary was so frightened by this violent attack that she howled inconsolably for weeks. Mom said, "I've got to see a pediatrician. I'm afraid that my little Mary is damaged for life." But after two weeks, Mom told the doctor and a Christian Science practitioner that her baby was beginning to calm down and taking small steps toward a normal childhood. To prove this story seventy-five years later, Mary points to the bare spot on her scalp from this traumatic attack. She can also recall being one of the most talented high school female singers being selected and performing in the prestigious LHS Women's Senior Octet. Later in life she earned outstanding teacher awards, two master's degrees in special education, and completed twenty-five years of being a beloved kindergarten teacher. With her thirty years of surviving breast cancer, raising two successful children with three precious grandchildren, I am thankful she was hardly damaged for life.

My parents' turbulent lives during the Great Depression and WWII, and living in five states (Nebraska, Pennsylvania, Massachusetts, New Mexico, and Maine) taught me much about the gritty American work ethic that comes into play in challenging environments—prairie, desert, farm, seacoast, and battlefields. Mom often affirmed, "Never let dust bowls, hurricanes, wars, or deaths stop you." If you work hard enough, get a good education, find a loyal spouse, become an effective employee, and live a faithful spiritual life, most Americans can succeed despite difficult barriers. Sadly, this was not the reality for African, Hispanic, Asian, Indigenous, LGBTQ, or disabled young Americans.

One example of my mother's personal sacrifice for her daughters was her taking a job at private girls' camps in Cornish, Maine, and Walker, Minnesota, for no salary in exchange for her daughters being able to attend these exclusive camps for eight years. By doing so she forfeited eight years of her Social Security benefits, which reduced her pension and lost her thousands of dollars from the ages of sixty-five to eighty-nine. Did anyone inform Mom that she should take the salary for her long-term financial security? Probably. "My girls' education comes first, and we can't afford the tuition at these camps. My girls will have only the best! They'll learn sailing, horseback riding, softball, and every sport these private camps have to offer!" Talk about selfless generosity. In this twenty-first century "Me First" era, how many parents would make such a sacrifice? At the camps I hit tennis balls on clay courts, and little sister Mary and I sang and acted in the modified Broadway shows the camp produced each summer (e.g., *Oklahoma, Show Boat,* and *South Pacific*). Imagine rough costumes constructed from outdoor gear in our suitcases. Imagine teenage voices squeaking to "Oh What a Beautiful Morning," "Old Man River," and "Bali Hai."

World War II ended in 1945 after more than 75,000,000 soldiers and civilians from all over the world had been killed due to massacres, war wounds, mass bombings, disease, starvation, and deliberate genocide. Five million innocent Holocaust victims had been exterminated—Jews, gays, disabled, Roma (gypsies), and Jehovah Witnesses. Many Holocaust civilians who were tossed in ovens were intellectuals, teachers, accountants, doctors, artists, composers, writers, and clergy. Japan surrendered after the atomic bomb built where Dad had worked in Los Alamos incinerated 220,000 innocent adults and children in Hiroshima and Nagasaki, Japan. The bombs burned the victims' bodies off so completely there was nothing but a pile of dust on the ground. Never again.

After his honorable military discharge, Dad returned to Portland, Maine, to join my mother and Mary Elizabeth and me at our home at 26 Codman Street. I was thankful he came home after so many had died on the European battlefields and in the Pacific. My father said, "I am worried if my job at the Fidelity Bank is still there. Thousands of us US veterans need work, and the competition is huge. I served my country and have a family to support." Unfortunately Dad did face many periods of unemployment. What I later learned as a WWII baby was gratitude for the 405,000 American men and women who gave their lives for peace and prosperity in my and my children's lifetimes.

Not only did several layoffs due to drinking on the job frustrate Dad, but the Army Air Corps' practice of serving alcohol in the field and on air bases had encouraged heavy drinking. As well intended as Ike's "happy hours" and the military's alcoholic culture were, these likely played a role in Dad's future alcohol addiction. Of course, seeing and smelling the decaying corpses of American soldiers and witnessing the slaughter of English and French children and civilians caused despair, addiction, and post-traumatic stress syndrome (PTSD) among thousands of veterans.

Gradually Dad found small jobs with Hudson Motors (an automobile manufacturer) and Nash Kelvinator (an auto and appliances manufacturer), while Mom did part-time secretarial jobs. "Even on our modest salaries, we will enrich our children's lives with trips to sandy ocean beaches, slippery stone quarries, beaming Maine lighthouses, local lobster pounds, and those pungent fish markets," Dad said to Mom. "Let's burn some maple leaves so our girls can later leap into the cool dry piles and we can all inhale their cherry scent!" Burning leaves was legal in the 1950s but no longer due to air pollution and accidental fires being started. Even today when I smell cherry smoke from a man smoking a pipe, my memory floats right back to my girlhood in Portland, Maine.

I was passionate about listening to Elvis's "Jailhouse Rock," Elvis's "All Shook Up," Little Richard's "Tutti Frutti," and even Johnny Cash's "I Walk the Line." And I was devoted to *American Bandstand* with its popular song "Rock Around the Clock," and jitterbug and boogie woogie dances, and of course poodle dog and pencil skirts. We thought we were so chic back then. I liked seeing Black and white kids dancing together, but no same-sex couples of course!

CHAPTER 3

Teenage Tensions and Grief

For the most part, growing up in Maine for us Pierce kids in the 1950s was full of many delights: pinecones crackling in the fireplace, cool ocean mist on our faces, mournful blasts of a distant foghorn, fish chowder with potatoes and onions, and fresh lobster Newberg sizzling in butter, milk, and cinnamon.

However, the deadly disease of polio ravaged our country until Dr. Jonas Salk and his team from the University of Pittsburg field-tested the Salk injection polio vaccine on thousands of us children. These children became immune to polio, and from 1953 until today, millions of American and foreign children thankfully receive polio vaccines. But unfortunately polio is back in Afghanistan, Pakistan, and even in some parts of the US: Orange County, California and New York City. Even when I traveled to Brazil and Argentina in 2023, the US Center for Disease Control and Prevention recommended I get the vaccine, and I did. So I am immune for the next hundred years!

In 2023 during the deadly coronavirus pandemic, the persons opposed to this cost-free, effective Covid vaccine were called "anti-vaxxers." Sadly, by the end of 2022, over one million Americans had died, often due to not getting vaccinated. Thankfully in the 1950s and 1960s, there was no "anti-vax" mythology rampant in the population. Think of the millions of children (like me) who would have died years ago of paralysis, amputations, crippling illnesses, and in iron lungs if anti-vax beliefs had been common.

My mother, a devout Christian Scientist, said she'd be the first in line to get her daughters vaccinated. And she was. The Salk vaccine of the mid-1950s might have saved the life of President Franklin D. Roosevelt who died ten years earlier in 1945. Dr. Albert B. Sabin in the 1960s further made the eradication of polio universal with an oral vaccine administered in a sugar cube. God bless all these scientists.

Meanwhile on Christmas Day in 1952, piles of red wrapping paper, gold ribbon, and silver icicles were strewn under the tree. Hoping there might be more, I reached under the tree and felt a silky warm object among the papers and ribbons. I saw a black-and-white kitten peeking out and jumped up for joy with a kitten in my arms. Every child wants a pet and I was no different. Today I've transferred from loving cats to being enamored with dogs. And I believe the adage, "To a dog you are the master; to a cat you are the servant."

Another great joy in Portland was shopping with Mom at the local fish markets. Grizzled Italian fishmongers wearing white aprons and shouting "certo" (certainly) tossed foot-long halibuts wrapped in wax paper to hungry customers. That was our "catch of the day." Other customers were arguing over the cost of haddock, mackerel, cod, herring, sardines, and tuna. The price of fresh lobster meat with no shell in the 1950s? Two dollars a pound. This fish market in Portland's Woodfords Corner, wet from salt water, seaweed, and fish scales, was the ideal place for me to skate around on smelly, slippery, slimy floors. Elsewhere in Maine, I loved seeing live lobsters boiling in giant black iron kettles; and at the shallow-water beaches, I had to be careful not to step on horseshoe crabs with their concealed spiked tails crawling along the ocean floor.

I loved listening to radio programs like *Our Miss Brooks, Jack Benny, Amos and Andy, Dragnet, Boston Blackie,* and the Boston Red Sox play-by-play. Sitting on the kitchen counter with our ears glued to the static from AM radio, my sister and I wondered who needs this newfangled gadget called television. Since our parents could not afford a television, we cried: "Do we have to drive all the way to the Hobsons' home in South Portland just to watch some *Ed Sullivan Show?* Boring! But wait, who are those cute guys from England called the Beatles singing 'It's Been a Long Day's Night'?" *I do kind of like them.* Certainly better than watching some dancing bears on *Ed Sullivan.*

I had many joyful pastimes nurtured by my dad's love of sports, history, the French language, politics, and geography. I became a lifelong history and geography buff as a teenager. As smoke from Dad's Camels wafted around me while I was eating Rice Krispies at the breakfast table, I read and discussed news and sports in the *Portland Press Herald.* Plus, I was mesmerized by Dad's war stories from England and France, particularly those of his military leaves in London and Paris. Dad told me I must see the Louvre, the Latin Quarter, the Arc of Triomphe, the Eiffel Tower, Big Ben, and Buckingham Palace. He taught me how to say "yes" and "thank you" in French (*oui, merci*), and I felt fluent. Later I wondered if I should major in French, which could include not just the language but the geography, history, art, architecture, and literature of La Belle France.

In addition to teaching me French culture, Dad directed me to focus on one sport when he bought me a dusty Maureen Connelly tennis racket at the Salvation Army. To upgrade and flatten the scratchy old racket, Dad brushed it off, screwed it into a broken wooden press, and said, "It is now brand new." We would read coverage of the tennis grand slam tournaments each season and even listened on the radio to the US Open. I now wonder, how did play-by-play tennis commentary sound? For me, it was "Have racket, will play tennis like Althea Gibson." It surely couldn't be too difficult—just grab the racket and start swinging. Wrong. I still strive to overcome bad habits as an adult.

Dad raised me like the son he didn't have by perching me on a red, banged-up, boys' Raleigh bicycle, pushing me as I swerved down Codman Street over gravel and cement cracks, and if I fell, he shouted, "Get up! Stop crying! Get a thick skin!" (Getting a thick skin became very helpful in my career along with "growing a backbone.") Next, he and I played baseball trying to emulate Red Sox star Joe Garagiola as Dad taught me how to grasp a cracked Louisville Slugger bat. One Saturday morning in our front yard, he said, "Let's play pitch and hit. I'll pitch baseballs to you and you'll hit them, got it?" Things were going well with several of my balls looking like home runs when one of them soared across the street, shattering the neighbor's front glass window. I started crying thinking how mad Dad and our neighbor would be and how I'd have to spend my meager allowance to pay for the replacement. But Dad said, "Susan, I am proud of how you hit that baseball, even though it did break the Paulsons' window. Let's go apologize and arrange to replace it."

When Mr. Paulson came out of his house, he said, "I was afraid of that loud noise thinking someone had been injured or killed in an automobile accident. Thankfully it's just a broken window. Ed, that girl of yours is a future Ted Williams. Accidents happen."

Still shaking in fear, I thought I was dreaming. I apologized to Mr. Paulson, shook his hand, and told him I would pay for his new window.

"Never mind, honey. I just wish my daughter would show some interest and ability in sports." And Dad did not reduce my allowance.

Also in my Portland, Maine, childhood years, my mother was ahead of her time among women, not only working full-time as a secretary, but also shopping, cooking, cleaning, and teaching Sunday school. "My daughters will have the best nutrition, the best K–12 education, and the best Christian education possible," Mom declared. Piano lessons and library cards? Check! Girl Scouts? Check. Outdoor exercise? Check. One day she announced, "We're driving to the Goodwill Store to buy you girls ice skates so you can glide, twirl, and jump like Sonja Henie on the Portland Evergreen Cemetery Lake." We drove to the lake on this sunny Saturday afternoon, and Mary and I put on our wool socks and slightly used white skates. And we were having a gleeful time even as we stumbled along as novice skaters. We were happy we lived close enough to the lake that we could go skating every week. I saw some school girlfriends, and we pledged to skate together every Saturday. After two hours we became tired and skated off the ice, removed our skates, replaced them with our boots, and waited for our moms to pick us up at 4:00 p.m.

While waiting for my mother a large dark-haired man in a rusty blue Ford drove up to me, rolled down his window, and asked if I'd like to see his puppy. I peered in, and all I saw in his lap was something that looked like a large, shriveled-up, gray sausage. The man kept rubbing it around and around and asked me to touch it. I was so frightened I ran as fast as I could to the parking lot where my mother and sister were waiting. When I told my mother what happened, she immediately called the police to report a pedophile who had exposed himself to a child. I learned to be more cautious before agreeing to do something unusual like looking for a "puppy." Such was the first sexual abuse in my lifetime, the first of my four #MeToo experiences. I shared this experience with my skating girlfriends so they could learn there are risks even in public and fun places. But this experience did not stop me from ice skating with my friends.

Despite many enjoyable enrichments, I hated another so-called enrichment. Our parents' daily commandment: School is number one in your life! "But other kids skip classes," I cried. I was forced into academics and proper behavior by strict teachers who wore orthopedic shoes, long skirts, baggy sweaters, and carried rulers to swat anyone on the wrist who misbehaved. I stood and recited the Pledge of Allegiance every morning, practiced choral music every day, and never missed my classes or homework in the three R's. With no record players, stereos, or iPods, music class was thankfully a requirement, not an elective.

"Only A's on report cards are acceptable," declared my parents. "Homework must be done before playing outside!" they commanded. This ethic actually served me extremely well for the rest of my academic life, although no amount of instruction helped me with algebra.

My active extracurricular education included French horn lessons aimed at imitating virtuoso Dennis Brain and attending Hebrew school with my classmate and lifelong friend Debbie. I even attended Hebrew School with Debbie and learned several words and expressions which I have since forgotten. Meanwhile, my sister Mary specialized in reading *The Secret of the Old Clock, The Hidden Staircase,* and every Nancy Drew mystery known to girl or boy.

At Haseltine Elementary School in Portland, proper decorum and dress were dictated per Emily Post and were equally as important as the three R's. For example, we girls were instructed to hold our plaid skirts tight around our hips while descending the creaking wooden stairs so boys on the lower floor couldn't look up and see our—oh, our underwear. Giggles galore. Boys wore L.L. Bean cotton slacks, belts, and white shirts with collars. No teachers would wear jeans in those days. Nor should they in these days in my opinion.

Teenage Tensions and Grief

I became an expert at the DONKEY basketball contest besting most boys on the school playground by shooting hoops like the Boston Celtics's Bob Cousy. In the DONKEY game, the shooter making the first basket required the second shooter to make the same basket or they would earn D if the second shooter missed. For example, if shooter A made a lay-up, shooter B would have to make a lay-up or A would earn a letter D; and the game progressed until one shooter earned all DONKEY letters and lost the game.

But this blissful adolescence couldn't last forever. Tensions and conflicts started disrupting my pleasant life in Maine. I was troubled at Maine Camp Moy-mo-da-yo with this strange jingling in my body each time I developed serious crushes on girls like Sally, a tall, tan, athletic brunette who was captain of my Green Team's softball team. Younger girls would sit with older girls when viewing the weekly movie (e.g., *Singing in the Rain* or *North by Northwest*), and I would slither discreetly toward Sally. I somehow felt I was "in love" with Sally even though I didn't know what love was at age twelve. Sadly, Sally ignored me, other than asking me to play left field on her varsity softball team. She feared the powerful sluggers on the varsity White Team, and she needed my help. I could catch fly balls in the outfield and had a .700 batting average, due to lousy pitching from the Whites. I was sure Sally would eventually notice and ask me to sit with her at the movies, but it never happened.

I also felt warm and "in love" with Becky, one of my cabin mates at the Maine summer camp. Becky, a shapely redhead from Boston with sparkling green eyes, liked to crawl into my olive-green Army cot and "practice hugging and kissing." I soon forgot about Sally. Becky and I got very good at hugging and kissing until one day after tennis lessons, the teacher caught us "practicing" (not tennis) in the bushes and scolded us for "unladylike behavior."

What's wrong with me? I wondered. I was afraid of my feelings for Sally and Becky, and even found myself lusting after the cute waterskier Pooky, the one with the bulging muscles and flowing blond locks. Pooky was straight out of Sunset Beach, and I was too nervous and shy to approach her. (Is anyone named Pooky anymore?)

Another type of serious tension my family and I survived in my teen years at home in Portland were the punishing 125-mph hurricanes that sounded like B52 bombers flying overhead. During Hurricane Alice in 1952, our small, white clapboard 1920 duplex rocked and rolled on its foundation while glass windows shattered like tinkling bells. Tree limbs slapped the roofs.

"Where are the flashlights and candles?" Dad cried.

"Is the cat inside?" Mom screamed.

"Where are buckets to catch streams of water?" little sister Mary yelled.

"Is Aunt and Uncle Charlie's Willard Beach home still standing?" I asked Dad.

"Should they come live with us?" Mom cried. "There are no live telephone lines so we can't even call them!"

When the hurricane finally blew out to the ocean, we wandered the streets looking at broken windows, downed power lines, cracked oak trees, and houses with their exterior paint stripped off. One mile from our house along Casco Bay, I breathed in the salt air and saw piles of lumber from shipwrecks that had washed ashore. Oil and gas barrels leaked black-gold into the harbor. On land, greedy rats feasted on piles of garbage.

I had another sorrow while growing up, which was enduring the shame of wearing hand-me-down clothes and being ridiculed for dressing like a "refugee from the Salvation Army." Our parents' rusty, gray 1940 Chevrolet and our alcoholic father passed out in our living room embarrassed me so much that I could not bring classmates home to play.

One of the worst of all the difficulties I endured in Portland, however, was sexual molestation by a fifty-five-year-old pedophile who was our friend Jeanie's stepfather. "Uncle Ted" drove the latest shiny blue Hudson sedan and let us steer the car while seated in his lap. But Uncle Ted's scratchy fingers molested our budding breasts and rubbed our soft, ten-year-old inner thighs. "Uncle Ted, stop that! It tickles and I don't like it!" I cried.

Uncle Ted replied: "I'm just being friendly with you, honey."

This behavior was illegal but steering a fancy car was such fun we girls tolerated this sexual abuse. I asked Jeanie, "Hey, what's that hard lump in Uncle Ted's lap? It must be part of the gears because he moves it around a lot." How naïve and innocent we were.

On one night when we spent the night at Jeanie's house, Uncle Ted drew the bubble bath water upstairs. While waiting for us to undress, he sat naked in the tub with what resembled a gray sausage floating on the surface. What's that? I wondered. Since clean bath water was scarce, all three of us little girls had to share the bath with him who slid his rough hands over my tiny breasts and private parts!"

I screamed, "Stop that," and jumped out of the tub yelling at Jeanie and my sister Mary to not get in that water with Uncle Ted! Meanwhile downstairs, Jeanie's mother, Aunt Nancy, was oblivious to what her husband was doing as she refilled her Scotch and soda. Our parents sincerely believed they could trust Aunt Nancy and Uncle Ted with their daughters, but on many occasions our dad was absent due to too many glasses of Jim Beam and our mom was cleaning our house. This sexual abuse by Uncle Ted and millions of other pedophiles may be minor compared to rape and female genital cutting, but all forms of violence against girls and women must stop in every country in the world.

Unfortunately, Dad and Uncle Ted had become daily drinking buddies. But despite the imperfect father I had and the criminal stepfather that Jeanie had, they often drove our families on scenic trips to the stone quarry near Westbrook where we hiked along the trails, picked blueberries, admired native flowers, climbed on trees and boulders, caught pollywogs, steamed clams, and ate a gallon of Friendly's chocolate ice cream. How outraged our parents would have been if they'd known about Uncle Ted's crimes. I'm sure these scenic trips with Uncle Ted and Aunt Nancy would have ended immediately. Not until the women's movement of the 1970s and the #MeToo movement of the 2020s did thousands of sexual abuse victims of all ages reveal their painful experiences with pedophiles, harassers, stalkers, and rapists. And even adult women in some countries perform genital mutilation of their young daughters. I understand that genital mutilation is done in some world religions, but would a loving God approve of this lifelong pain, depression, and post-traumatic stress disorder (PTSD) for thousands of girls and women?

There were many more joys in Maine including visits to the Hobsons' house on Willard Beach in South Portland. Young Alberta Hobson was Dr. Albert Haskell's first and only cousin, and when Albert died, she became Mom's adopted sister. Our "Aunt Berta" was a black-haired, adventurous math graduate from Bates College in Lewiston, Maine. The US Navy's WWII colorful recruitment posters had tantalized her with ARE YOU A GIRL WITH A STAR-SPANGLED HEART? JOIN THE WAVES! (Women Accepted for Volunteer Emergency Service). Nationwide, over eight thousand young women immediately signed up as lieutenants junior grade (LTJG), and later eighty thousand more enlisted as WAVES. I'm proud of my role model Aunt Berta who served the war effort as an accountant and mathematics specialist in the Portsmouth Naval Shipyard on the Maine–New Hampshire border.

Visiting the Hobsons on the Atlantic Ocean brought many thrills: watching the seagulls screeching and diving for fish and wading in the bay to cool our sunburned feet. We feasted on Aunt Berta's homemade whoopie pies, a Maine specialty concocted of two saucer-sized chocolate cookies filled with whipped cream. Aunt Berta's father, our Uncle Charlie, would roast corn on the cob while live lobsters boiled in a black iron pot.

But the highlight of visiting this family was watching their black-and-white TV on Sunday nights. Mom and Dad couldn't afford a TV, so every Sunday night we motored across the South Portland Bridge to the Hobsons to eat lobster swimming in butter, or sometimes halibut fish chowder made with onions, corn, and salt pork. Watching the highly anticipated *Ed Sullivan Show* was a highlight with its dancing bears, flying trapeze artists, and some small musical group from England called the Beatles. How thrilling it was to not only hear singers and comedians on the radio, but to see them on television, albeit through the constant blinking "snow" on the screen. A huge "invention" in the late 1950s was a red, white, and green plastic cover to place over the black-and-white TV screen—and voilà, we had color TV. We decided that this new machine called television had its assets but was much less imaginative than listening to the radio where we could draw our own pictures.

Did the lack of a television in the Pierce household present a serious handicap for us girls becoming popular and culturally literate? "Yes! Unfair! Everybody has a TV! Everyone else gets to watch *Howdy Doody!*" we cried. Another friend who was also deprived of the spectacle of television was my sixth-grade classmate, Debbie. A doctor's daughter, she lived seaside on Baxter Boulevard in the "high rent district," while the Pierce sisters lived on the wrong side of the tracks on Codman Street. Debbie's parents dictated, "No playing outside until homework is done, only A's on report cards are acceptable, Hebrew school and French horn lessons are required!" I was blessed to have been charged with high academic and social expectations that have served me well for my entire life. These parents gave me the courage and ability to go out into the world to fix things that are wrong. Today Debbie and I meet once a year in the Roxbury, Connecticut area where she and my daughter reside. Debbie and I do lunch and brag of course about all of our gifted and talented grandchildren.

Instead of gorging on TV intellectuals like Tiny Tim and Peewee Herman, Mary and I were forced to examine all thirty musty volumes of the *Encyclopedia Britannica* in the Portland Public Library, to read every newspaper and magazine in the home, i.e., the *Portland Press Herald, Life,* and the *Saturday Evening Post.* Then there were the mandates to listen to Chopin and Beethoven on the radio, to practice piano as taught by a buxom retired opera singer, and to play softball in the streets. "Go out, ride your bikes, and practice your math at Bernie's Corner Grocery, and get going now!" bossy parents demanded. Now at Bernie's store, for only five cents, I could buy my choice of one dill pickle fresh from the green brine in the oak barrel or one Devil Dog, a chocolate hot dog bun bursting with vanilla whipped cream. My ultimate delicacy was the deep-fried vanilla cream puff with cinnamon sugar for a pricey ten cents. And I considered the red wax lips that I placed in my mouth to be so very fashionable.

With no television at home, I was forced to use my brains and body to win the cowboys vs. Indians battles with neighborhood kids. At the Christian Science Sunday School, I studied Bible stories and Mary Baker Eddy's *Science and Health with Key to the Scriptures.* Our young voices soared to hymns from "Joyful, Joyful, We Adore Thee," set to Beethoven's "Ode to Joy" and to the Christian Science favorite, "Shepherd, Show Me How to Go." Mary Baker Eddy was not only a gifted religious leader and author but also a composer of hymns; she took forty traditional melodies and paired them with contemporary lyrics.

Like her colleagues Susan B. Anthony and Elizabeth Cady Stanton, Mrs. Eddy represented the strong "uppity women" who incurred the wrath and ridicule of most ministers and politicians of the late nineteenth century. Neither Eddy, Anthony, nor Stanton lived to see the results of their lifelong commitment to the passage of the 19th Amendment in 1920 guaranteeing women the right to vote, nor did Eddy live to see Christian Science becoming an international religion or the *Christian Science Monitor* becoming a worldwide newspaper of record. (The *Monitor* is now a biweekly international magazine full of much good news from all parts of the world.) Today we are standing on the shoulders of these great women who shape my beliefs and inspire me to fight for what is right and to fix things that are wrong.

Not all of my early life took place in Maine. My enterprising and clever mother booked seats on the Penn Central Railroad in order to expand two wide-eyed daughters' horizons in New York City and Pennsylvania. How could Mom afford such railroad trips on her part-time salary and with an often-unemployed husband? Apparently as a very frugal woman, she had saved enough to take us girls on this trip. I wanted to see the world—cities, towns, and farmlands. I was thrilled to see the precision dancing of the athletic Rockettes and the drama of the Academy Award–winning film *Mr. Roberts* at the Radio City Music Hall in New York City.

I was honored to meet my Uncle Harry in Erie, Pennsylvania, who was a tall, slender man wearing bifocals. He was a WWI veteran who served as a medic in France and explained the horrors of trench warfare, poison gas, and tanks from 1914–1918. I can't imagine the gruesome injuries, diseases, and deaths that Uncle Harry witnessed in his job that killed and injured over 116,000 Americans. This was a war with a total of 14,000,000 military and civilian casualties. He motivated me to study armed conflicts throughout history, and I became a history and geography buff for life.

Mom, Mary, and I drove off to the farmland in Mercer, Pennsylvania, to meet our maternal grandfather, Edwin R. Hosack, a dairy farmer with bulging muscles and a long, snowy-white beard wearing blue bib overalls. Sadly, our maternal grandmother, Mary Daugherty Hosack, had passed away earlier at age seventy-one. She was Irish (emotional), and my grandfather Edwin was Scots Irish (stingy). So I owe my very strong emotions to my Irish descent, and my miserly behavior to my Scots Irish heritage. My daughters Mary and Annie have called me outspoken, emotional, stingy, and a tight wad. Okay, I do get emotional, but I'm not a miser. I'm just frugal.

At our Hosack grandparents' family farm near Mercer, I picked strawberries from bushes and apples off trees, I jumped in haystacks, picked eggs out of the hen house, smelled and fed the oinking pigs, and tried my hand at milking cows. Not as easy as it looks! Teetering on a small stool, I squeezed, pushed, and pulled the nipples while aiming clumsily at the milk pail in the barn. But all I ever got was a single creamy drop. On the other hand, our chubby, curly-haired Uncle Bobby, sitting on a stool and whistling "Yankee Doodle Went to Town," squeezed so well he could hit thirsty horses' mouths ten yards away.

And I learned to ride a horse. Mom's sister, Aunt Mimi, was a tall, tanned cowgirl who also gave me rides on her brown and gold palominos. She drove a red truck like the Marlboro Man with a cigarette dangling out of her mouth. Things looked perfect on this farm, but Grandpa lamented, "We're losing our dairy business due to the strip mining for coal. It's shearing off the hills and poisoning our land, water, air, and livestock. How are we small farmers going to make a living on this sacred land, which was deeded to us two hundred years ago?" I had never considered how important clean land, air, and water are to the survival of human, animal, and agricultural products all over the world.

CHAPTER 4
Moving to the Wild West

"What do you mean we're leaving Maine and moving to . . . where? Dad's native Nebraska?" I cried to my parents in 1957. This was the worst news I could ever imagine: leaving New England, my beloved Hobson and Zolov families, quitting the junior high school marching band, and moving to the Wild West. "I hate Nebraska! There'll be gunfights in the streets and savage Indians attacking our house, just like in John Wayne movies," I cried.

Dad had lost jobs in Maine and couldn't support our family. In Lincoln, our new home, he applied for several jobs but was not hired for any of them. My mother needed a job to pay the rent and buy food and medical care for us. She met a neighbor who worked in the Lincoln Public Schools (LPS) who encouraged Mom to apply for any secretarial job in the district. Mom had considerable secretarial experience in Portland and Boston, and after several rejections she did win a job in the English office.

After a year of surveying the culture and the organization, Mom proposed a literacy project to her English supervisors. Mom was determined to build more support for pupils to learn reading, a most important skill. Although not college educated, Mom had a lot of common sense and informed her supervisors that "looking at this reading data, too many of our children are failing the Iowa Test of Basic Skills and they are not making adequate reading progress." She courageously suggested to her supervisors an important vision: "Lincoln students will learn to read so they can read to learn for the rest of their lives."

The directors agreed and organized many services for the teachers on proven ways to teach reading (phonics and phonemic awareness), which gradually improved students' scores. Then they promoted Mom to a high-level administrative position. I learned from Mom's determination and courage (speaking up to bosses), when something is wrong and not working, fix it.

To help his family, Dad explained, "Even though I lost jobs in Maine, my sisters Dorothy and Mary here in Lincoln will help me find a job and get established." And they did, finding us a rental house near Aunt Dorothy's tree-lined Tudor mansion on C Street. I was twelve years old, and Aunt Dorothy Pierce Russell was a pillar of demands. Standing five foot six, stout with brown eyes and curly brown hair, she was an English teacher, songwriter, and mother of four who insisted that her niece, me, arrive at her home every Saturday morning at 9:00 a.m. to lecture her on how to become a perfect student and a perfect lady. I believed a modern-day Professor Higgins had appeared in the form of my aunt Dorothy, and I was the clueless Eliza Doolittle, indoctrinated just as my own mother had been by her big sister Kate.

Aunt Dorothy wore long black brocade gowns and black ballet slippers and blew out clouds of smoke while swirling around her silver lorgnette like Joan Crawford. With her head circling high and low, left and right, she banged on her Steinway piano, "I'm in Heaven When I'm with You," forcing me to read the music and sing along.

Sipping butternut coffee, she pointed her long finger at me and dictated the Plan for My Life: "You will speak up, plan ahead, grow a backbone, and earn straight A's in school and in college; you will fix things that are wrong, matriculate at the University of Nebraska; you will pledge Kappa Kappa Gamma or Delta Gamma, *never* Theta; you will earn a teaching degree; you will find and marry a rich man, preferably a Phi Delt; you will bear and raise his children; you will join the Lincoln Country Club and the Junior League, buy season tickets to Nebraska football, and never miss a game; and then you will live happily ever after. Voilà, my dear!" she chirped excitedly.

With that, even at age twelve, I fearfully saluted Aunt Dorothy, considered her dictates but disagreed with several of them. What's a country club? What's a Phi Delt? As it turned out, I disregarded some of her plans but believed I would have the ability to graduate college and to fix things that were wrong.

Six years later when I enrolled at NU, I learned Dad's other sister, my Aunt Mary Pierce Mahn (nicknamed "Mano") was the housemother at the Kappa Kappa Gamma sorority house on the NU campus and another stickler for earning nothing but A's. OMG! Mano made sure those Kappas were studying night and day and earning good grades. Thus my sister and I were surrounded by demanding parents and aunts with ridiculous orders and expectations for us. Not fair.

It is difficult for young children to get established in a new city like Lincoln, and especially challenging for low-income teenagers like my sister and me assigned to a "country club school" of all places. As a newcomer I entered Irving Junior High School dressed in drab brown, Mennonite-type attire acquired from the Salvation Army—nothing like the chic Pendleton plaid wools, tweeds, and cashmeres worn by the rich girls.

The very first question we newcomers were asked by every female member of various cliques was "What legacy are you?" By "legacy" they meant daughters, granddaughters, or nieces of sorority alums. I quickly found myself black-balled by the Theta clique, the Pi Phi clique, the Kappa clique, the Delta Gamma clique, and the Tri Delt clique. Being ostracized by the Irving cliques and other elitist classmates meant I often sat alone in the cafeteria and had no one to play with or walk with to school.

When riding my rusty blue bicycle to school, I was often taunted by chubby, nasty bullies who harassed me and pushed me off my bike into the busy street or onto cracked sidewalks. "Girls shouldn't ride bikes!" they jeered. After several attempts to pedal to school, I gave up and walked one mile each way, even with frozen fingers in blinding blizzards or sweating in searing humid heatwaves.

Any newcomers at Irving JHS like me were labeled losers. However, I thankfully found another "loser" named Ginny Wheaton with whom I ate lunch. Ginny had moved to Lincoln from New Jersey, and we became fast friends. But speaking of lunch, what is this food in Nebraska they call "lunch"? Fritos, chili, sloppy joes, fruit cocktail? Please, no! Where were the Boston baked beans, brown bread, and fish chowders?

Meanwhile, was my attending this country club school a total disaster? Not entirely. Enter Miss Tillie Larson, English teacher dictator, five foot four, 130 pounds, age fifty-five, with a mop of frizzy blond hair and Coke-bottle style glasses dangling off her nose. When she interrogated you, her chubby fingers gripping her wooden cane, you saluted and squeaked, "Yes, ma'am!" Anyone who misbehaved received a rap on the wrist from her cane. It was just my misfortune that Miss Larson and my bossy Aunt Dorothy were NU classmates and both fanatics for all aspects of the English language: ideas, organization, grammar, punctuation, spelling, vocabulary, fluency, word choice, voice, cursive penmanship, and diagramming sentences ad nauseum. *Whatever is this diagramming for,* I mumbled. It forced me to map out subject, verb, object, modifiers, clauses, and those tiny, worthless prepositions. What a waste of time! Or was it? Today, when I am in a grammar jam, what do I do? Okay, I remember how to diagram.

Thankfully, Ginny and I survived Irving JHS, enrolled in Lincoln High School, and were able to attend the same geometry class. We telephoned each other every night about solving syllogisms. And I loved syllogisms—so orderly and logical. Through our joint homework efforts we even became lifelong friends. She understood the pain of leaving one's birthplace. We both excelled in French and delighted in listening to Dad's WWII war stories and to Ginny's mother's vaudeville stories.

Ginny's mother, Rosie Wheaton, was another blessing for my family and me. Rosie had curly, silver hair and was the talented chief organist at the large Plymouth Congregational Church in Lincoln. Rosie had acted in vaudeville and Off-Broadway productions for twenty years. She insisted that we girls join the school choir and band and attend classical and sacred concerts with her and my mother. I once asked Rosie how to play the organ, thinking it looked like fun, sounded powerful, and I might try it. Wrong. It seems that an organ has twenty pipes, five manuals, 346 ranks, two keyboards, and a wind system. My organ career was over before it started. Then Rosie told me an interesting fact—the largest church organ in the western world is the one at the Cadet Chapel at the United States Military Academy at West Point, NY, and weighs 124 tons! Since organ was not in my future, I learned to play the folk guitar, which was hugely popular in the 1960s and the 1970s. But listening to the organ in *Phantom of the Opera* or in sacred music always gives me chills.

Ever so eager to please the influencers in my young life like my parents, Debbie's parents, Aunt Dorothy, Aunt Mano, and Miss Larson, I labored like a coal miner to avoid dangling participles or using the objective voice when the subjective was correct. Our adults commanded us to *never* show "low-class breeding" by abusing the King's English.

Then one day in class Miss Larson gripped my shoulder like an iron clamp. "Susan, you will become a writer, understand?"

But I protested, "Writing is tedious and painstaking and I don't have time!" Miss Larson objected. "You seem to have plenty of time to play tennis and softball, so I never want to read a weak essay from you below a grade of A, or I'll report you to your aunt Dorothy and she'll quarantine you on weekends to practice writing." Miss Larson's dictate to become a writer has echoed in my mind for over sixty years, and this teacher from hell smiles down on me as I type these words today.

Having previously believed I had a somewhat perfect life, I was surprised when I suddenly started experiencing an anger and despair that tore me apart. When hormones started raging in my adolescent years, they raged not for boys, but for girls like Sally, Becky, and Pooky at Camp Moy-mo-da-yo. And this inclination toward girls instead of boys kept getting stronger. Problem. What was wrong with me? I just didn't understand what was so thrilling or fun about boys. I had loved playing sports and dancing with boys, but no more. Stop flirting with me. Let's be friends. No kissing please. Many good slumber parties were ruined by boys showing up. Friends reassured me that I would learn to love them. Maybe I could become a "practicing heterosexual"? Keep practicing. Just forget those silly feelings toward girls.

But how could I have fun socially while avoiding boys? After all, they were 50 percent of my fellow students. *Got it!* I could engross myself in extracurricular activities like chorus, Girls Athletic Association, pep club, recreational tennis, the National Honor Society, and a part-time job at Lincoln Telephone and Telegraph (LT&T). No time for boys now. Thank God I could avoid those gropers and growlers. In the meanwhile, since there were no other girls who felt as I did in Nebraska or in the entire country, I decided that I was just "different." Listening to Robin Morgan, Barbara Jordan, Gloria Steinem, and Bella Abzug a decade later, I became a feminist, learning that it might be normal for girls to love girls and for boys to love boys. Okay, it's called gay.

But boredom with boys was the least of my pain and suffering in my adolescent years. In May 1966, my father tearfully informed me that my first cousin, Mary "Sis" Russell O'Shea, had been raped and strangled to death. *This can't be true. Dad must be drinking again. Wrong.* In disbelief I wondered what kind of a man would commit such a heinous crime against a thirty-six-year-old mother of four who was married to a prominent businessman and lived in an exclusive Lincoln neighborhood? A yard man and drifter from Denver, Thomas A. Alvarez had attacked Sis when three of her children were at school. When she fought his amorous advances, he pinned her down, violently sexually assaulted her while her two-year-old son was napping and finally strangled her, leaving her dead on the cold, linoleum kitchen floor.

This grisly crime greatly upended my Pollyanna view of life. *Oh, there's evil in my world?* I wanted to know why isn't life fair? How can I deal with grief? How do the families of victims overcome hatred and the desire for revenge toward the killer? Do they ever forgive the offender? I know I hated this man sentenced to life in the "Old

Max" Territorial Correctional Facility in Canon City, Colorado, and later sent to the Sterling, Colorado Penitentiary. I believed the death penalty should have been his punishment. Or would life in prison without parole be worse? I wondered.

My parents, sister, and I grieved, but what about Sis's parents, husband Teddy, and her four children? How do you tell little children that their mother is dead and they'll never see her again? Sis would never experience the joy of seeing her children graduate high school and college, succeed in careers, marry lovable partners, and enjoy the thrill of grandchildren. She lies alone in a cold, windswept plot on the Lincoln prairie, while her killer enjoys forty-nine years of all the "benefits" of prison: three meals a day, a safe roof over his head, a paid prison job, full medical and dental care, visits from his children and grandchildren, and even conjugal rights with his wife. What remorse, if any, does he have? I need to check if he is still alive and consider meeting him and forgiving him. One lesson learned for me is that girls and women should protect themselves by not letting a stranger into their homes even if they are there to help in the house or yard.

At that time, I believed he deserved the death penalty, but I have since changed my mind about this sentence after learning it doesn't deter crime; some offenders are wrongly accused and executed, and it costs millions of taxpayers' dollars for public defenders, endless appeals, and lawsuits. I also question whether Colorado and other states should be in the business of state-sanctioned murder?

While trying to shape successful lives, Sis's four children struggled growing up without a loving mother: job insecurity, their uncle's suicide, their father's and stepmother's accidental death in a blazing house fire on Christmas Eve, and their grandparents' deaths in old age. Then tragedy struck again forty years later when Sis's oldest daughter's husband, piloting a five-seater Cessna, accidentally lost control of the plane in a blinding rainstorm. The pilot, his twelve-year-old son, his elderly father, and a friend died immediately as they crashed on a Minnesota wheat field. Was the plane overweight with fishing and camping gear? Or did it run out of fuel after flying beyond its maximum range of six hundred miles? How much grief could Sis's daughter or any person take? Despite all these losses and heartbreaks, Sis's four adult children have managed to live honest and productive lives.

Although nothing compared to the rage I felt at my cousin's violent death, another source of anger in my teen years was my burning distress that girls were barred from playing high school sports. At the time I didn't know what discrimination was; all I knew as I gritted my teeth in my high school principal's office was that something was wrong, and I and others would fix it.

Where did I get such audacity? It all started with my friend Ginny Wheaton with whom I shared a love of sports; but at that time, girls were barred from playing high school sports under federal, state, and local rules. High school coaches informed us that girls were too weak and fragile; they needed to protect their reproductive organs. Representing athletic directors' opinions of girls playing sports, the Commissioner of the Colorado High School Activities Association Commissioner, Glenn Wilson, wrote in 1955, "We do not favor girls' athletics on the same basis as boys as a spectator sport. We are very strong for having intramural girls' athletics and also having play days for girls." Play days? No way! Intramural sports are not enough! *I'm going to fix this,* my naive, determined fifteen-year-old self proclaimed. But when, where, how, and with whom?

Fortunately, at least there was one competitive club sport for girls in Lincoln: softball. A civic-minded grocery store owner Mr. Martin, with little knowledge of softball himself, did gather enough girls to make up a team to play in a city-sponsored girls' league. He provided the equipment and uniforms. The city threw out a few balls, bats, and gloves, and suddenly we had a team and a game. Thank you, but where do we learn to catch, throw, hit, field, and pitch? Sorry, no coaching provided. But boys' baseball teams had all of this instruction of course.

My classmate Ginny turned out to be such a natural slugger that my dad nicknamed her "Wheatie" as in "Wheaties: Breakfast of Champions." That nickname sticks to her to this day. I was the impatient catcher who coaxed and cajoled our pitchers to just get it over the plate. We on the Martin's Team needed an adult coach who would train and teach us the softball skills instead of just throwing out a ball and a bat.

Then one day in July my parents told my sister and me that we were going to learn to play tennis. I had learned a little tennis in Portland but barely enough to even get the ball over the net consistently. My parents didn't have money for all the equipment and apparel that tennis requires. But Mom had met Mr. Win Elman at church and heard he played tennis at the Lincoln Tennis Club (LTC). She asked him how her girls might learn to play this lifetime sport. This was back in the day when parents watched their children like hawks and channeled them into healthy activities. Win Elman was a tall, handsome, tanned, prominent Lincoln lawyer and a confirmed bachelor. (Could the term "confirmed bachelor be an euphemism for "gay") He drove a gold Cadillac convertible and played tennis with a group of local priests on the LTC clay courts. He decided to pay for our new Head tennis rackets, Wilson tennis shoes, fuzzy yellow balls, court fees, and even gave us a roll of dollar bills for our A&W frosty double root beer floats after playing on those humid, ninety-five-degree days. "How lucky are we that the A&W is right across the street from our courts!" we cried.

But one thing missing from Win's generosity were lessons that taught the forehand and backhand topspin, and the strong core body rotation essential to maximal power on the court. The topspin grip and stroke enable the ball to bounce high above the opponent while bouncing in on the very back line. I'm stuck with a pathetic slice, which in later years I've tried to correct with not much success. But learning to play tennis as a youngster in heat and humidity gave me an advantage because I am rarely distressed by furnace-like conditions in my tennis games. All I have to do is "keep the ball in play," which is the number one commandment in tennis. Then I can watch my opponent melt down in the sun and the steam. Okay, it's called "winning ugly."

Recently I was fortunate to hear and watch my eight-year-old granddaughter being taught the tennis topspin, which regrettably I never learned. If I had learned this at age eight, I would be consistently a better player. And you're never too old to learn new skills! Tennis has taught me outstanding life skills: I am fairly fit and strong, and I have many friends with whom to enjoy friendly competition. Who needs to be number one when being an average player brings such joy?

In addition to softball, Wheatie and I played tennis of course at the LTC, but we often had to first rake and roll the wet clay, paint the white lines, and raise and stabilize the heavy damp net before hitting any balls. In winter we even shoveled snow off icy, concrete courts. How crazy was that? One day a tennis coach at the LTC asked me if I would be willing to hit some balls at the NU indoor court with Althea Gibson of all people. Gibson was the first African American who had won several Grand Slam tournaments like the French Open in 1957 and later at Wimbledon and the US Open. I thought there must be some mistake for a kid like me to play a world champion.

Out on the court, most of her shots went flying past me, but I was able to hit a few past her. I had developed a passion for tennis, playing with the enthusiasm of a Billie Jean King and a Serena Williams, but I never won any trophies until later in life in some adult leagues. All I learned from tennis was joy, competition, strength, and a can-do attitude that has propelled me throughout my entire life. Pete Sampras who won numerous Grand Slams really nailed it when he said, "Tennis uses the language of life: service (as in 'serve'), advantage, fault, break, and love."

CHAPTER 5

Higher Education and New Teacher's Blunders

After my dispute with the LHS principal, Mr. Bogar, regarding girls' unfair exclusion from high school sports I was still thinking, something is wrong and I am going to fix it. I know what I will do! I will matriculate at the University of Nebraska to become a lawyer and fix discrimination against women, girls, African Americans, Hispanics, Indigenous, LGBTQ, and disabled people. But I abandoned this goal based on societal pressure at the time for women to become teachers, nurses, secretaries, and unpaid mothers. Those were our options. And my LHS counselor advised me that because of my good grades, I should aim higher than being a secretary. I heard her say, "Become a legal secretary!" I still wanted to attend law school, pass the bar, become a practicing lawyer, and win cases for my clients.

With no encouragement from the adults in my life to attend law school, I decided teaching sounded good to me—I could become a French teacher, enjoy working with young people, travel to France, have summers off, and be able to supplement a potential husband's income. With my goal now set for a college education to become a teacher, I certainly needed a job to pay for tuition, books, and supplies. My father and mother generously offered to pay for my room and meals. I was fortunate that my Sunday School teacher with connections to supervisors at Lincoln Telephone and Telegraph (LT&T) told me that LT&T was hiring summer telephone operators for ninety cents an hour! "Wow, a job for me, what a miracle," I cheered, "but what are these split shifts?"

They were killer shifts. For example, one was 9:00 a.m. to 1:00 p.m. and then 5:00 p.m. to 9:00 p.m. Desperately needing a job but very annoyed with the hours, I asked, "What do I do during that break between 1:00 p.m. and 5:00 p.m.?" That meant the "workday" would last over twelve hours! I guess I'll spend those four hours in the public library studying for some class I haven't enrolled in yet. A better decision, however, was reading favorite classics like *Grapes of Wrath, Main Street, Babbitt,* and *A Room of One's Own.*

I was thankful to learn the skills of a telephone operator including developing a pleasing disposition and valuing working long hours to meet customers' needs. While sitting in the company's cafeteria on breaks I was dismayed at many veteran operators talking only about their irritating husbands and disobedient children while they puffed on Pall Mall cigarettes. I was dreaming higher than getting married and raising children. I was convinced that I did need a college degree to become a teacher and possibly a lawyer. I decided teaching is truly a most noble profession. And I felt grateful to my parents who sacrificed owning a home, a new car, and annual vacations so their daughters could achieve the American dream of a college education.

To keep my sanity at the phone company, I managed to find humor in this very social technical job. For example, when a rural farmer called asking for the telephone number of a Joe Yazchariensky, I asked, "How do you spell that?" He said, "J-O-E." Thanks a lot. Some weird men would call and say I had a pretty voice and how would I like a "fun night" on the town when I got off work? Sorry. Ladies would call to ask what time does *Breakfast at Tiffany's* start at the Strand Theater? Other callers asked for the phone number of the Corn Chowder Hotel, or the Corn Custard Hotel. They meant the storied Lincoln landmark Cornhusker Hotel.

Thanks to my parents and LT&T, I was able to pay for my BS degree and make a good living and lifelong friends. For example, my LHS friend Ginny Wheaton and I at NU both pledged Sigma chapter of Kappa Kappa Gamma sorority, the chapter Ginny's grandmother helped found in 1910. Another NU Kappa best friend, Patty Knapp Tweed, coached me through French, history, and political science at NU, Judy Erickson Gaylor was the friendliest of the Kappas from that snooty "country club" Southeast High School, and she and I became best friends, even sharing the same birthday, except that she is ten hours older than me.

Kappas gained an unfair reputation of being snobs, but at NU we had no time for superior attitudes because for us, academics ruled. The Kappa grade point average must be 4.0 every semester. "Live for the GPA!" our senior sisters demanded. Of course, not all of them could boast a 4.0 every semester either. In the 1960s in Nebraska, I was mostly oblivious to the civil rights movement and the opposition to the Vietnam War. For me activism and protests were secondary to studying for my classes and maintaining my best GPAs. My Kappa academic life consisted of (1) study halls, (2) cramming for tests, and (3) sitting in the front row of classes to ensure that I would pay strict attention and my professors would notice me. The Kappa upperclassmen admonished us younger ones to "Keep your GPA up to make sure those Thetas don't win the Highest GPA Award again."

But after academic priorities, there was plenty of fun in the 1960s Greek life: singing Kappa and folk songs, hootenannies, blind dates, coke dates, panty raids, gossiping while in a long line waiting for a telephone booth to open up, keg parties (called keggers where we all drank beer), "woodsies" where women and men would drink beer and kiss (and do other things) out in the corn fields, pinnings when a sorority woman became "promised" to a fraternity man, playing bridge, NU football games, and all-nighters when we crammed for tests to keep the Kappa house GPA up.

And to keep up our nightly energy, we awaited deliveries from the Nebraska classics Valentino's Pepperoni Pizza, and Runza's Cabbage Rolls, which are made with crumbled spicy hamburger, grilled onions, and melted Swiss cheese. In those days, "watch your weight" was not a commandment for young women. But my mother in heaven still preaches to me to "just take one cookie, Susan." Sorry, Mom.

Each year, the university awarded prestigious honors to the Greek houses that scored the highest GPA. How shameful it would be for the Kappas if we didn't win! "Don't YOU be the Kappa who brings down the house average," the Kappa officers admonished us. Best friends Patty Knapp Tweed, Ginny Wheaton Hallager, Sheri Jacobsen Roos, and Judy Luhe Farmer were the geniuses who brought our House average up with their 4.0 averages. Me? Not so great—maybe 3.5 on a good semester.

Of course, housing curfews ruled in the 1960s. All college women were required to be inside their dorms and sorority houses by 10:30 p.m. Sunday–Thursday, midnight on Fridays, and 1:00 a.m. on Saturdays. Breaking curfew resulted in being locked out, parents being notified, and demerits being amassed that could bench a coed for the next weekend, month, or year. No alcohol or men were allowed in houses and dorms, but smoking cigarettes was okay.

One year we all smoked two packs of Marlboros per day in order to win a cheap black-and-white Motorola TV. How healthy was that? We were required to wear dresses and skirts in all classes and on campus, and at every Monday sorority evening meal. Paradoxically, smoking in stuffy classrooms was permitted, but not outdoors or on campus! We were instructed to wear our Kappa key pin only on dresses or sweaters but *never* on a T-shirt or sweatshirt. The senior officers explained: "Never return to the house with Pabst Blue Ribbon or Boone's Farm wine on your breath. Breath mints don't fool Housemother Mano." Of course, no such rules applied to fraternity or dorm men.

Committing any type of social faux pas could get you a TAK ("That Ain't Kappa") reprimand announced at Monday night dinners in front of 125 frowning sorority sisters. The number one TAK: Failure to stand up when an alum or other adult entered the house. Number two TAK: Wearing pants to class. (I frequently broke #2 by keeping jeans concealed under a drab tan London Fog trench coat.) Although all these rules were intended to protect our image, the Kappa officers thought nothing of us dancing in our blue flannel nightgowns every Saturday morning on our front lawn across the street from three fraternities.

Speaking of fraternities, I had difficulty getting excited about dating fraternity or other men. Now I wish I could have dated attractive, intelligent NU coeds. Given my ambivalence about dating the other sex, I dedicated myself to academics and organizing Kappa socials. Serving as the social chair and one of the song leaders provided me good excuses for not dating campus men very often. Since I knew of no NU women who wanted to practice hugging and kissing each other like I'd done with Becky, my summer camp girlfriend, I decided I would happily live the single life. I never connected my attraction to girls as being gay because "gay" was never in my vocabulary or brain. I'd never even heard that word in the 1960s.

I will never get pinned, engaged, or married. I'll have a fabulous career somewhere—without a husband I promised myself. Kappas not pinned or engaged at graduation time were labeled "old maids" and were required to suck lemons at a "fun" end-of-the-year luncheon. Now I wonder if "old maid" was a euphemism for "lesbian," but I'd never heard that word either. The expression "women like that" probably meant gay or lesbian, but there were probably no "women like that" in Nebraska or Maine where I had lived. Shortly before college graduation, I saw on a coed's T-shirt a quip that said, "A woman without a man is like a fish without a bicycle." I thought there may have been some truth to that.

But seriously, shouldn't I at least try to find a fiancé at NU as Aunt Dorothy the Dictator had ordered? So, I made the decision to become a "practicing heterosexual," but with no kissing, hugging, foreplay, or sex. I dated hundreds of handsome NU men. With three men to every one woman on campus, it was easy to get dates to athletic events, concerts, mixers, and movies. I dated presidents of fraternities, football stars, and BMOCs (big men on campus). I was elected second vice president of the NU Student Union, which allowed me to meet some of the best guys that NU had to offer. But I had no intimate feelings for these "good catches," as they were called. A rich handsome rancher from Valentine? Sorry. A cute pre-med student from Scottsbluff? No. A future president of the Omaha National Bank? Not so much. I loved dancing with them and talking geopolitics and sports, but they always seemed to want something more. I asked myself, will something click if the right one comes along?

Sadly, on November 22, 1963, our lively academic and social lives were abruptly shattered when the black-and-white television channels interrupted bridge games, classes, and study halls at 11:00 a.m. to announce that the president of the United States, John F. Kennedy,

Jr., had been shot and assassinated in Dallas, Texas. In shock and disbelief, we gathered together with tears in our eyes for the next forty-eight hours with TV anchor Walter Cronkite. We all sobbed. Our hero and young leader was dead? Surely no one would murder such a talented and dedicated man. How could there be such hatred and insanity in the world? Thus ended what we thought would be a normal and peaceful rest of our lives. How naïve and wrong we were.

Despite our grieving of the JFK assassination, life had to go forward. After graduating from NU in 1964, Patty Knapp Tweed, Judy Erickson Gaylor, and I set forth to what we thought was the most glamorous city in the USA. "Cowtown Denver," as it was affectionally called, had teaching jobs at $4,900 a year, lots of single white men, snow-capped mountains, sexy ski outfits, margaritas, enchiladas, a mild climate, and proximity to our Nebraska families. Perfect. But why didn't I even think about single white women or women of color to date? Heterosexuality was so pervasive I never had an opportunity to meet any gay women, let alone date one. I certainly lacked "gaydar," although today, gaydar is not real reliable due to the emergence of "lipstick lesbians," lesbians who look like straight women with long hair, makeup, and the latest fashions.

My first job in Denver in 1964 was teaching French 1, French 2, French 3, and seventh grade World History at Byers Junior High School at 150 South Pearl Street. Still today, the building and grounds near Alameda and Washington streets resemble a stately Oxford campus with ivy-covered towers and immaculate gardens. The only thing that struck me as strange about my new job was my heavy nightly preparations of four lesson plans!

But when I reported for duty on my first day, my principal informed me of another "little assignment" as he called it. "Susan, you'll have blind students in your three French classes. These students are very bright and will do very well! No problem for you." No one had told me when I was hired that Byers was a magnet school for the visually impaired. What training had I ever had in teaching the blind? Fortunately, the district provided a sighted blind specialist to translate my worksheets, songs, and readings into braille. And these students did have such acute hearing that they could pronounce the French language as well as the native speakers they heard on the French reel-to-reel tapes.

In Denver one roommate, Judy, landed a job as a physical education teacher and was appointed as the cheerleader sponsor at Wheat Ridge High School, a perennial high school football power. How ironic that I have resided in Wheat Ridge for twenty-two years. Judy was an athletic, charismatic, blond educator who had been the homecoming queen at Southeast HS in Lincoln, Nebraska. Roommate Patty, with her 4.0 GPA in political science and the highest GRE (Graduate Record Examination) ever recorded at CU-Boulder was a cute, energetic brunette who found a low-level accounting job with the Denver Water Department. Brilliant academic women like Patty were rarely hired for high-level jobs due to gender discrimination.

As SWFs (single white females) we assumed that we would find hundreds of SWMs in outdoorsy Colorado. Again, I was so clueless I never considered dating gay women because I didn't know what gay was, and even if I did, where would I find them? So clueless and naïve. Soon in 1966 Judy married a business teacher, Harry Gaylor from Lincoln; then Patty, whose family owned a summer home in Minnesota, married a handsome auto mechanic Gary Tweed from Pequot Lakes, Minnesota, in 1969. I married US Navy LTJG Don Schafer from Lincoln, Nebraska, after his brother Norm had introduced us. Not knowing if I would ever meet or date a gay woman, I shrugged those hesitations off and loved Don as a brother.

Obviously we single women had decided that the home boys were the safest bets for loving husbands and fathers. And they were.

But before dating and getting married, I thrived as an inspired teacher for five years at Byers Junior High School, named for the first editor of the historic *Rocky Mountain News*. Byers drew students from the Denver Country Club (DCC) area, so along with my academic duties, I was also charged with escorting Byers students to expensive French restaurants, like Lafitte's in downtown Denver, and chaperoning them on trips to Europe in 1967 and 1968, with their parents paying all of my expenses. (I didn't take students on a foreign trip until after I'd traveled to Europe in 1965 and 1966, which I will describe later.) These 1960s pupils were not seeking alcohol, drugs, or sex, so there were no discipline problems for me. My only challenge was surviving the long days from 7:00 a.m. to 11:00 p.m. as these energetic teenagers and I toured ancient monuments from the Louvre to Notre Dame to Big Ben to the Colosseum. Clearly I was becoming a history and geography buff for the rest of my life.

I was seriously blessed to meet at Byers a powerful role model in the person of Mrs. Kate Stonington, a mother of five children including one of my Byers students. Kate was born and raised in New York City and descended from Robert Livingston, one of the signers of the Declaration of Independence. She had short brown hair, a sturdy, tanned, athletic body, a hearty laugh, and a wide smile. She became a leader in the Denver League of Women Voters and the Denver Democrats. As a wealthy woman who could have been a socialite if she had desired, Kate instead was engaged in school desegregation battles, civil rights, and efforts to stay out of the Vietnam War. Playing bridge poolside at the Denver Country Club and spending time in small talk was not Kate's idea for the best use of her many talents and life.

Having lived in Maine and Nebraska where Republicans were the majority party, I'd never met a Democrat. Kate Stonington inspired me early on to work in progressive politics for social change and justice. She modeled for me how to use one's education and intelligence for the good of people and for children at risk. On any day at her solid brick house on a tree-lined avenue in old Denver, I met people who needed help finding a job and affordable housing, accessing medical care, or securing a college education.

Kate was there for foreign students, racial minorities, and immigrants, and used her vast knowledge of public benefits to lift people up who were less fortunate than she was. I saw what a life of servant leadership looks like: using one's ability and education to help the less fortunate, to mend fences, and to seek bipartisan support of critical local, state, and national problems. This servant leadership was one of the most important lessons I've ever learned. Sadly Kate passed away at the young age of sixty-six, a huge loss to her family, friends, community, and to me. She exemplified the power of a role model, and everyone would be blessed to have someone like her in their life. And her memory is a blessing for me.

My earlier mission of "Something's Wrong—Let's Fix It" surfaced again during my first year at Byers. The Denver Public Schools foreign language curriculum did not permit any foreign language reading or writing instruction to be taught in the first semester; only listening and speaking instruction were allowed because that's how infants learn a language. I believed this was wrong, but did I dare approach my boss, the district's foreign language supervisor Madame Cheval, an imposing woman who wore her red hair coiled up in a bun on top of her head? I wanted to tell her that junior high school students are not infants!

Higher Education and New Teacher's Blunders

I didn't want to get fired in my first year of teaching, but in order to expedite my pupils' learning, I believed they should learn all of the language skills simultaneously: listening, speaking, reading, and writing. So I decided to secretly supplement my instruction with what I determined to be a common-sense approach, hoping Madame Cheval would not find out. Fortunately, she did not, and my students often earned some of the highest marks on district French tests. And I was teaching French without actually having traveled to France yet.

During my first trip to France, I learned this lesson of teaching all four skills of reading, writing, listening and speaking. Unlike the Denver schools, NU had gone overboard with emphasizing reading and writing but severely limiting instruction in listening and speaking. With no common conversation skills despite my four years majoring in French at NU, I made a very embarrassing blunder one day. I asked a garage station attendant, "*Où est la salle de bains?*" (Where is the bathroom?) He and his friend laughed hysterically as they pretended to lather up their hair and bodies with sponges and soap suds. I should have asked, "*Où est la toilette?*" (Where is the toilet?) Thanks, NU, for never teaching us French majors the most needed and basic phrases.

So when my students traveled to France, I made sure they could converse using slang and street language and included such necessary skills as counting French francs, making change, finding a toilet, reading and navigating the métro, and ordering food from menus. And they were able to read and write postcards home to their families.

Another very embarrassing mishap occurred after a huge dinner with my fellow French Sorbonne students as I was rubbing my stomach and proclaimed, "Oou, je suis pleine." They threw up their arms and laughed hysterically. What had I done? Instead of saying, "I am full," I had said I was pregnant. For weeks after this disaster my classmates would ask how many pounds I had gained, did I have morning sickness, and was I eating a lot of liver so I would certainly bear a very healthy baby?

Thankfully I was able to teach my Byers students common mistakes tourists make in France. And after sixty years since my students and I traveled to France, four of us still meet once a year for margaritas, guacamole, and enchiladas at the Table Mountain Inn in Golden, Colorado. (Not exactly French cuisine.) We reminisce about sailing in the *bateaux mouches* on the Seine, about admiring the historic châteaux in the Loire Valley, and our first sips of café au lait with warm buttery croissants. These four youngsters, who somehow aged and are now retired, represent an era when joy and laughter ruled in schools instead of high-stakes testing and active shooter drills.

One particular memory we chuckle over was my strumming my folk guitar in the French classroom, which was right next door to the venerable teachers' lounge with a Do Not Enter sign on the front door. Inside were teachers on their planning period, puffing on Lucky Strikes, and debating union politics. And most of them were not thrilled with the sounds of thirty eighth graders joyfully chanting and clapping to "La Marseillaise," "Alouette," and "Napoléon Avait Cinq Cent Soldats."

I also remember the raging debate in the lounge in 1964 about whether female teachers should earn the same amount of money as male teachers. Congress had just passed the Equal Pay Act of 1963, but it was controversial: many citizens still felt women should earn less "because they'll all get married and have husbands to take care of them." Really?

To Denver Public Schools' credit, by 1964 male and female teachers earned the same grand starting salary of $4,900 per year. I felt so rich that I bought my first extravagance that year for $1,900, a 1964 forest-green Volkswagen sunroof Beetle. To prove I was really cool, I clamped a ski rack on the bug even though I didn't know how to ski.

Another misadventure and near disaster I caused on my first trip to France in 1966 was overlooking a major detail involving my travel partner. My NU friend Norm Schafer and I had decided to travel together once we arrived in France, but we were unable to go over together because I'd already made reservations on the German cruise liner Bremen. So we decided to meet at the pier in Cherbourg at 4:00 on June 25, 1966, when the ship docked. We assumed the Bremen would surely never dock at 4:00 in the morning, but just in case we were wrong, we had the sense to make a Plan B: If there were any problems, we'd meet at the Cherbourg Post Office.

And wrong we were. At 3:30 a.m. on June 25, the mighty Bremen blasted her mournful foghorn, alerting all debarking passengers to rise and prepare to dock. Waking in terror, I nonetheless believed Norm would correctly figure out the arrival hour because he was smart. He was a NU medical student! Wrong again, and there I was—it's pitch black and raining, and I'm by myself at the dock at 4:00 a.m. There were only twenty other passengers out of six hundred who debarked, but they all spoke German and quickly jumped into getaway cars. Sadly, I saw zero sign of Norm, no waving of French flags, and not even a BIENVENUE EN FRANCE sign. (Welcome to France.) After walking the half-mile down the slippery, dark pier, dragging my fifty-pound suitcase, I spied a tiny lightbulb dangling over the figure of an elderly longshoreman who lay dozing in a folding chair. What could I say to him at 4:00 a.m. on this, my first day in France? What good did all those years of studying the subjunctive and Balzac do for me? All I could think of was "I'll never trust Norm again, and where in the world is the Cherbourg Post Office?"

I managed to stammer my first question in French to the dock worker: "Où est la poste?" (Where is the post office?) and he replied, "Oùvert à neuf heures." All I understood was "neuf," which means nine; the post office must open at 9:00 a.m.! But it was only 4:00 a.m., and how could I find it? The second question I squeaked out was just one word: *Taxi? Taxi?* "Arrive à sept heures" he grunted. Seven. Trying to gather my composure, I thought, *It's now twenty degrees on this windswept coast, and—oh no, I have no money! I need money for a taxi.* What was the French currency? *Oh, oui, yes, the franc! Yes, I do remember the franc. But where do I get one? Could I give the cabbie a $20 traveler's check? Will he have change for $20?* But of course, there were no taxis at 4:00. After shivering, slumping, and weeping on my behemoth suitcase until 7:00 a.m. when a taxi finally arrived at the dock, disaster was confirmed: no Norm! Terrified, I was a single naïve young woman alone in a dark strange country.

Thankfully the cabbie accepted my $20 traveler's check, and I received several silver, red, and blue bills and some copper coins in change. Now, what do I do at a foreign post office at 7:00 a.m.? Sitting on a bench outside the post office, I looked around and spotted an elderly white-haired woman pushing a straw broom across the cobblestone street in front of her apartment. A sign of life! I watched a lively seaport waking up: burly fishermen shouting "*Allez!*" (Let's go), shutters flying open, and a few bistros owners hanging out "*Oùvert*" (Open) signs. There goes a priest—*please pray for me.* Wish I could find a gendarme. Did I dare buy a café au lait across the street where I'd have to speak French? *Un café au lait?* (Thankfully, I remembered the French national beverage of choice.)

Gathering my courage, I ordered a *petit café au lait* with a fresh almond brioche and, miraculously, paid for the first time with French francs. I felt so culturally competent! At the post office, the sympathetic postal clerk gave me several sheets of thin Aéropostale paper with which to write a letter. But to whom? Yes! My mother would be so happy to hear what a wonderful time I'm having here on my first day in la Belle France.

I was certain Norm would be arriving soon as I was sitting and writing on the hard, wooden bench for seven hours . But by 5:00 p.m., no Norm. No Norm at 6:00 p.m. And the post office was closing, night was falling, but who was that giant bedraggled Anglo guy struggling up the street dragging a huge canvas bag? Norm! We cried, embraced, and stammered our survivor stories, and celebrated that at least we were in France and that we had found each other. After our harrowing trips we wanted to drink a bottle of Saint-Emilion and gorge ourselves on onion soup, crusty baguettes, and boeuf bourguignon at the petit Café du Nord down the street.

Needing a place to sleep, we searched around the dark village and located a tiny Hôtel de Mer and decided we must share a room to save money. The bespeckled proprietor with gray hair and gnarly hands looked dubious but didn't ask if we were married. American hotels in the 1960s did not rent to couples "living in sin." But apparently in France, anything goes. Vive la France.

CHAPTER 6

An Ugly Yet Hopeful World

Norm and I triumphantly rode the Société National des Chemins de Fer (SNCF) train to Avignon, Provence, and Nice before I started summer school at the Sorbonne University in Paris. The American Association of French Teachers provided reduced tuition and housing for six weeks to teachers attending summer school at one of the world's foremost universities. *Quelle chance*! What luck! But before arriving in Paris, however, Norm and I committed several embarrassing faux pas. One day we bought a quarter pound of the smelly, marbled black-and-blue roquefort cheese, which we innocently left in our warm, breezy hotel room while we went sightseeing the next day. Upon returning to the hotel we gasped at this stinking odor emanating from the second floor down to the lobby. If other guests called us ugly Americans, we deserved it. This rotting roquefort scent had permeated the entire establishment, and it was so foul and suffocating in our room we couldn't sleep that night. Sightseeing and navigating on ancient, narrow, slippery cobblestone streets is challenging enough even when one is operating on seven hours of sleep; but on two hours of sleep, we lost not only respect among angry fellow hotel guests, but we lost a day of seeing gothic cathedrals, Roman aqueducts, and street artists exhibiting their floral oil paintings.

We committed another faux pas by overindulging in tomato and brie salads, chocolate éclairs, and those warm escargots sizzling in garlic butter. We both experienced a few GI problems, especially after Norm had eaten four piles of fresh Marseille mussels causing him to spend the next two weeks searching for "toilettes" every few hours. I admired the magnificent Provence region which is truly God's country: fields of lavender waving in the breeze and releasing their perfumed scents, and azure-blue skies gently rolling over deep green seas. I noticed fields of grape vineyards, which meant the pricey Dom Pérignon champagne existed only in my dreams, but every little café served *vin rouge ordinaire*, which would fit my modest budget and actually tasted quite good.

Upon arriving at the Sorbonne in Paris, I was required to speak formal French in class but to use French slang on the street. I learned in two weeks what I should have learned in four years at NU. My father had told me stories of the horrors of World War II, but hearing about them from our professor was shockingly brutal. Our white-haired, black-robed Sorbonne professor wearing a large Christian chain had barely survived the German occupation in Paris. As a little girl, she could not find her family, had no place to live, and depended on strangers to find shelter and food.

Now a grandmother at age seventy-two she painfully described how her aunt, uncle, and two cousins in the village of Oradour-sur-Glane near Limoges, France, had been locked inside a church on June 10, 1944. She said that the Nazi Waffen-SS Panzer Division poured gasoline all over the building, torching it into a blazing inferno that incinerated 142 innocent men, women, and children. A total of 643 adults and children were rounded up and locked in other burning buildings, all perishing in the Oradour-Sur-Glane Massacre. Ninety-nine percent of the residents of Oradour were murdered. On February 26, 2023, the *New York Times* reported that the last survivor of the massacre, Robert Hébras, had died at the age of ninety-seven in St. Julien near Oradour. Although Hébras was shot and severely injured, he'd survived only by falling under hundreds of dead bodies.

The Oradour ruins are now a memorial site, but why the Nazis had chosen this peaceful small town is unknown. The painful stories from WWII never end and even to this day in 2024 massacres are occurring in many countries. In February 2022 Russia invaded the peaceful sovereign nation of Ukraine accounting for thousands of deaths on both sides. Such a waste of soldiers, civilians, children, homes, land, schools, hospitals, and historic buildings and churches. Fifty years after hearing my Sorbonne professor's story of her relatives' deaths, the horror of war in any land makes me ask, "When will the human race ever become the humane race?"

I wonder, if women ruled the world would things be more humane? Would conflicts be negotiated instead of destroying land and killing people? I learned about the Iroquois Haudenosaunee Confederacy located in upstate New York and in North America in which lives a tribe of Indigenous nations including the Mohawk, Oneida, Onondaga, Cayuga, and Seneca. When I visited this area of upstate New York and Seneca Falls in 2022, I learned that the early American suffragists and feminists of the 1800s based many of their goals on the Haudenosaunee (pronounced ha-don-ah-son-nee) Nations' rights for women, which American women had not yet won—the ability to vote for the chief or president, holding elective office, winning custody of their children, owning property, keeping the wages they earned, punishing any man by prison or execution who committed violence against a woman or child, and negotiating conflicts with enemies instead of picking up weapons. The Nation's spiritual beliefs proclaim the sacredness of both women and the earth because they both create life. Thus any violence against women and the earth in any form are unthinkable and immoral, wrote Dr. Sally Roesch Wagner, a Haudenosaunee scholar.

Certainly in France, which has survived thousands of years of armed conflicts, I was fortunate one sunny Saturday morning in Paris on July 14, 1966, to watch, smell, and hear the festivities of Bastille Day. This holiday celebrates when an angry mob of protesters stormed the hated Bastille Prison on July 14, 1789. This attack signaled the beginning of the French Revolution. I walked to the Arc of Triomphe and watched the huge French Army, Navy Royale, and Maritime Coast Guard proceed three miles down the five lanes along the Champs-Élysées. I smelled gun powder, fumes, and smoke; I heard military bands playing "La Marseillaise" and saw soldiers, flags, tanks, amphibious vehicles, and handsome gendarmes on horseback. Thousands of citizens and tourists lined the streets waving tricolors as French Air Force jets screamed overhead leaving contrails of red, white, and blue. I felt like I was a part of world history too as I considered the many armies that had marched triumphantly down these hallowed cobblestone avenues.

I studied centuries of French history, geography, language, cuisine, and culture at the Sorbonne, which deepened my respect for people and customs across the world. I was overjoyed riding the métro through Paris, strolling through the Musée d'Orsay and the Luxembourg Gardens, listening to concertinas and chanteuse Edith Piaf singing "La Vie en Rose" and "Je Ne Regrette Rien." I loved browsing the many bookstores and art galleries on the Left Bank, and of course, dining on the best steak au poivre and pommes frites in the world. In 1966 for only three dollars (fifteen francs) you could buy a full meal (*prix fixe*) that included wine, soup, baguette, entrée, and dessert. My favorite museum in Paris was the Jeu de Paume, known for its collection of Impressionist masterpieces located next to the Place de la Concorde. I learned that this collection is now housed at the Musée d'Orsay, a former railroad station. After my six weeks in France, I was armed with the best photographs, popular songs by rock star Johnny Halladay, and my embarrassing disasters to share with my Byers students.

My friend Toni, a fellow French teacher, and I took a trip to Paris, which became a huge and painful "lesson learned" experience for us. As clueless tourists, Toni and I believed the invitation told to us by two young, handsome Frenchmen we met strolling down the Boulevard St. Michel at dusk. "Hey," they said, "we are doctors, we drive Mustangs, and we want to take you lovely ladies on a date! We'll have a nice dinner, wine, and then go disco dancing." Sounds good. But at the end of the evening, they expected us to return to their apartment: "Come on, we want to get to know you better," they said. When we objected, they forcefully pulled us out of the bar and tried to push us into a taxi. (Where was the Mustang, I wondered.) We ran down the Boulevard Saint-Michel in our high heels and miniskirts screaming, "*Au secours*" ("Help!") and thankfully hid behind a uniformed gendarme holding a nightstick. "You rich Americans, you cheated us and you owe us money for dinner and drinks," the "doctors" yelled at us. The gendarme guarded us as we hurried down several blocks to our apartment, with the "doctors" following and shaking their fists at us. In my Sorbonne class the next day, I learned that the most common pickup lines used by French hustlers were "I am a doctor" and "I drive a Mustang." My Byers students loved this story about their clueless teacher, but also it was a lesson learned for me and for them.

Such sexual harassment was no joke, then or now. It leads to rape and sexual violence around the globe. Male prerogative in all parts of the world ranges from sexist jokes, stalking, and touching, which can lead to sexual assault, rape, and death against females as young as four and as old as ninety. Sexual harassment became a crime under the US 1964 Civil Rights Act, which gives women protection from sexual harassment, but the law is not self-enforcing. Unless a girl or woman files a lawsuit against a perpetrator, he will likely continue this hateful and hurtful behavior, and still today sexual harassment and abuse are common and gender violence is still rampant in the US and most other countries. Often victims do not report the abuse for fear of retaliation by their offenders, employers, or from their families.

I wonder how we can fix sexual harassment and violence from occurring in the first place. What if large organizations that attract millions of men and boys sponsored a program called "No Assault on Women" or "We Support Safety for Women" or "Courtesy for Women, Guys." Leaders more creative than me could develop some catchy slogans that would encourage men to reconsider violent behavior before harming a girl or woman. Such organizations as the National Football League, the National Basketball Association, the Automobile Association of America, the American Medical Association, the US Olympic Committee, and the Boy Scouts of America are largely composed of men who could cause men to rethink their behavior before striking or hurting a woman or girl. Okay, call me too idealistic and unreasonable, but our society has to do something to prevent sexual harassment and assault.

CHAPTER 7
Marriage, Motherhood, and Sexism

After that frightening sexual harassment incident in Paris with the "doctors," I felt much wiser and returned to the United States. The best upshot of my friendship and previous trip with Norm was later being introduced in 1967 to Norm's younger brother, Don. Don was six foot two and handsome with sparkly blue eyes and a gentle smile. I was somewhat smitten. Could this be the man I might marry? Don was a civil engineering graduate from NU and was from a respected Lincoln family. He became a US Navy pilot flying A-6 Intruder jet bombers off aircraft carriers in the South China Sea during the Vietnam war. This A-6 jet flew at night to destroy roads and bridges when the enemy's surface-to-air missiles were less likely to hit and destroy the A-6 and other American aircraft. For Don's bravery and accomplishments, he earned the DFC, the Distinguished Flying lostCross, which is one of the American's military highest honors. Sadly some of his pilot friends lost their lives in this Vietnam lost cause.

I returned to Denver to teach school, and Don had some leave time from the Navy, so he and I started dating. We organized my busy teaching schedule with Don's Navy schedules to arrange dates in Denver. Since Don was a bit shy, after one and a half years of fun and romantic dates, I decided I would like to marry this wonderful man. So one night after drinking and dancing, I got up the courage to propose marriage to him. (How brazen of me!) And he said yes!

A few months later, I resigned from DPS, Don received three weeks of leave, and we married on March 29, 1969, at the Lutheran Chapel on the NU Campus. The chapel was filled with friends, family, lilies, roses, and an organ playing hymns and "Here Comes the Bride." After the service, friends threw rice over us as we sped off to Aspen for a skiing honeymoon. Later we were assigned to San Diego Naval Air Station (NAS) for one month, then to NAS Oceana Virginia Beach for four months and later to NAS Whidbey Island, Washington, for two years. I found a job at a community college on the island and enjoyed the life of a Navy wife, especially the birthday parties for adults and children, and some tennis matches and bridge games with other wives.

I was surprised one day on Whidbey Island in 1968 before Don and other pilots deployed again to Vietnam. Don told me: "Flying is fun and I think you would enjoy becoming a private pilot." Who, me?? No, thank you! Don had heard about the women's rights movement and encouraged his wife to sign up for flying lessons. "Women can fly and do a lot of things," Don told me. "A small single engine Cessna 180 can be rented for $40 an hour, and an instructor for only $50 an hour on this naval air station. So just try one lesson!"

"NO WAY!" I screamed.

I was very frightened but reluctantly decided to try it, but just once. My sixty-year-old, grizzled instructor, Hank, wore a Red Baron flying scarf, wrinkled jeans, and a black T-shirt that read CAN'T GET NO SATISFACTION as he chewed tobacco. I had zero confidence in Hank. Why would I risk my life with this so-called flight instructor? Something's wrong here, and I will fix it by dropping out of this death mission ASAP! But I didn't want to disappoint Don, so dubiously I boarded the small plane whose call number was November 35 or N35 for short. "Flying is easy," Hank said. "It's just the landing that's difficult." Yes, I would want to land.

The first lesson covered the parts of the plane and how to use the instruments. "Just push the stick forward (that thing that looks like a gear in a car), steer with your rudder (that thing on the floor that looks like car brakes), get your airspeed up to 500 miles per hour, keep your eyes on the altimeter (that horizontal bar on the dash board that shows you are flying straight and won't tip too far right or too far left), and gently lift the nose up to level off at 1,000 feet," ordered Hank.

I decided: Okay, this is scary but fairly easy with Hank at my side. And what a sense of power! With hands shaking on the stick, I managed to glance out of the rattling plastic windows to see the puffy white clouds over the San Juan Islands, pods of orcas, bald eagles nesting in evergreens, and kayakers gracing the shorelines. To the east, the lush green Olympic rainforest trees swayed in the breezes. To the west were thousands of miles of the Pacific Ocean. All was good, and I was actually enjoying flying an airplane. Who, me? Yes, I was even having fun.

Soon my one-hour lesson was up and it was time for the dreaded landing. Hank quipped, "I could land with my eyes closed . . . but I won't." I actually did land the plane with help from Hank. The next lessons entailed learning and practicing smooth landings. "These are not for amateurs; don't try these alone," advised Hank. "For landing, just locate the airfield and landing pattern, cut your airspeed, radio the controller, tell him you're November 35, ask which runway number he wants you on, keep your nose up, and gently put her down so your tires hit the ground."

The next lesson included putting the plane into an intentional stall, also known as the death spiral. But why in the world would I intentionally put the plane into a death spiral? Hank explained, "Just in case you ever encounter severe turbulence, bad weather, and you accidentally roll over and lose power, you'll know how to recover from a stall."

Ten lessons later, I almost felt like WWII flying ace, Jimmy Doolittle, gracefully making smooth takeoffs and landings, and recovering even when pesky crosswinds swirled and blew N35 dangerously off the runway near the grass and mud. Practicing landings is called a "touch and go," and I found it fun to show off my aviator finesse. Fortunately, I could avoid death spirals by flying only in good weather, and I earned my private pilot's license in 1972 by passing the written test and completing forty hours of solo flying. As I landed after my fortieth hour, the ground crew came running out to cut the back of my shirt off, an old airplane tradition. Maybe the expression "flying by the seat of your pants" without a shirt acknowledges the tradition of flying somewhat indiscriminately but safely. Women are allowed to keep most of their shirt minus a small square cut out from the back; men lose their entire shirt.

However, novice pilots like me do encounter frightening situations. Once before I passed the forty hours of solo flying I flew into a cloud bank at 3,000 feet with no visibility ahead, behind, down, up, left, or right of my aircraft. I wasn't trained on using instruments, and I panicked when I couldn't see usual visual landmarks like a bridge, a highway, or an ocean. Would I collide head-on with another plane? Relying on my belief in God, I cried, "God, please help; I know you're here with me!" Truthfully, I heard a booming voice shout, "Climb!" and then I later recalled Hank's instructions that when you are lost and cannot see, aim up, and climb, climb above the clouds several hundred feet higher for better visibility. It was God instructing me to not panic, just climb, climb, climb.

I had another death-defying flight at a rural Washington airfield where I needed to do just a "touch and go." However, the windsock (a large white cloth showing which direction the wind is blowing) was twisting and turning in all directions, and I couldn't see which direction on the runway I should "touch and go." Should I fly in a circular motion from the southwest around to the northeast, or from the southeast around to the northwest? Whichever way I did it, I was proud of myself that I had managed to land my N35. Upon landing, however, several men from the airfield office came running out, waving their arms furiously and yelling, "You almost caused a head-on collision with another pilot by flying in the wrong direction!" Naturally I was ashamed with the disaster I almost caused and decided to never fly when the weather was even a bit inclement or I couldn't see the direction on a windsock. Even though I had checked the weather report to confirm that all was clear on that particular day, clouds move in quickly, not just over the Pacific Ocean area but everywhere.

When Don and I were stationed on the Pacific and the Atlantic coasts, we enjoyed combing warm beaches for seashells, listening to squawking seagulls, and glimpsing giant spouting whales. The massive *USS Enterprise* and *USS Constellation* aircraft carriers took my breath away: 5,000 sailors on a floating city, each carrier weighing 95,000 metric tons. Although I somewhat understand the physics of how a heavy load displaces water, it still seems impossible that carriers don't sink.

Fifty-eight thousand Americans died in the Vietnam War, and their names are enshrined on the Vietnam Wall in Washington, DC. The carnage in South and North Vietnam was two million civilians, one million North Vietnamese soldiers, and 250,000 South Vietnamese soldiers. Looking back, did the United States stop the spread of communism, which was the purpose of the war? Since 1972 the Socialist Republic of Vietnam has been a socialist/communist country.

While Don was serving another tour of duty in Vietnam, I had retired from teaching and had enrolled at the University of Colorado at Boulder in 1969 to pursue a master's degree in counseling and psychology. I thought how fun this would be: climbing the jagged Flatirons foothills, skiing on weekends, enjoying ivory tower discussions with other graduate students, and becoming an expert on Freud, Skinner, Maslow, and Carl Rogers. Wrong. With traditional American norms being discarded by the churning turmoil of the 1960s and 1970s, I found myself caught up in protests against the hated Vietnam war but in support of Black civil rights, equal rights for women, gays, and the disabled. And I was horrified by the hallucinations and deaths from psychedelic drugs. I had enough trouble thinking and remembering anything without drugs, plus they were illegal. Could someone convicted of using these illegal drugs have a future as a counselor or psychologist? Of course not.

While I was a graduate student at CU from 1969 to 1970, the free love movement spread a lot of venereal diseases and caused unintended pregnancies and future abortions. The 1969 Woodstock Festival in a farmer's muddy field in upper New York state was not as glorious as advertised: many people experienced drug and alcohol overdoses, and some even died. Although many participants at Woodstock greatly enjoyed the experience, I failed to see the thrill of thousands of naked festivalgoers listening to Joe Cocker and Janis Joplin while making love in rain-soaked tents. Janis had an electric stage presence belting out songs like "Get It While You Can" and "Down on Me." Joe was very popular when he sang "You Are So Beautiful" and "Let's Go Get Stoned" with his raspy voice.

Later, cities and college campuses were burned and bombed by demonstrators protesting the assassinations of President John F. Kennedy, Dr. Martin Luther King, Jr., Senator Robert F. Kennedy, and Malcolm X, all positive, strong leaders whose goals were crushed by their premature deaths. On May 4, 1970, the National Guard murdered four young students and injured nine others at Kent State University in Ohio, further undermining public trust in our law enforcement, the military, and our government, this distrust lasting to this day.

Meanwhile in 1969 in Harlem, New York, in Marcus Garvey Park, the Summer of Soul peacefully featured Black singers, dancers, bands, and civil rights orators to celebrate Black Power and the Civil Rights Act of 1964. Unlike Woodstock no lives were lost, no women were raped, and there were no drug overdoses. Alcohol consumption was kept to a minimum because Black children were singing with the bands. Rev. Jesse Jackson preached the gospel, and performers like Gladys Knight and the Pips, Stevie Wonder, and Mahalia Jackson performed and uplifted the crowds for six weeks.

While I was still in graduate school at CU, President Lyndon B. Johnson seized the moral high ground to push for passage of the landmark Civil Rights Act of 1964: discrimination based on race, color, sex, religion, and national origin was prohibited in employment, housing, education, and public accommodations. This was no small accomplishment, given the prejudice at the time against Black people, largely from racist leaders like Governor George Wallace of Alabama, who shouted "Segregation Forever!" in a bullhorn at the Montgomery State Capitol. Later at the University of Alabama, he delivered his hateful "Standing in the School House Door" speech where he blocked two Black students, Vivian Malone and James Hood, from entering a high school. JKF ordered the National Guard to protect these teenagers as Malone and Hood walked timidly yet courageously through the high school's iron front door. How frightened they must have been with angry crowds, snarling dogs, thick fire hoses, and police officers with guns threatening them. These students are national heroes in my opinion.

I was greatly troubled by this political unrest and knew that something was wrong, terribly wrong, and needed to be fixed but how? I could see that societal problems extended far beyond my exclusion from high school and college sports. Thousands of Americans were dying in Vietnam; Republican President Richard Nixon ordered crooks in 1972 to break into the Watergate Democratic Headquarters in Washington, DC, and then he resigned from office in disgrace. Millions of people of color were struggling to find jobs, food, housing, medical care, safe neighborhoods, and public education.

There at CU-Boulder, numerous "radical" ideas were being debated by women's and gay rights speakers: writer Gloria Steinem, US Rep. Bella Abzug, gay writer Robin Morgan, NOW President Ellie Smeal, and Boulder professor and psychologist Dr. Marjorie Leidig. I was inspired by an article that Leidig wrote titled, "How to Become a Famous Feminist." To me, that was a goal worth pursuing—not to be famous but to do much good to educate and lift up girls and women. Through all this upheaval I worried how my husband, Don, still serving in Vietnam, would view this anti-war chaos.

At CU-Boulder I met Judith G. Nelson, a fellow counseling graduate student from Minnesota, who, like me, was working on a master's degree (MA) in counseling and psychology. I thought Judith was very strange because she wore bulky blue leather shoes called clogs that looked like you could wear them to clean out stables. How clueless I was. Now clogs have become comfortable and ultra-chic. Judith was a blue-eyed, strong, curly-haired Scandinavian with whom

I drank bourbon sours in clandestine cafés. Judith and I discussed my recent marriage and my frightening growing attraction toward women instead of men. At that time, I'd never met any gay women. I told Judith that all gay women lived in Greenwich Village, New York City, and certainly not in Nebraska, Minnesota, or Colorado. Judith and I both denied that we might be gay, and I even advised her to get married, have babies, and live happily ever after because being gay would be an extremely difficult and possibly dangerous life.

When I confided in one of my counseling professors that I was having fears that I might be gay, he said he could help me process my thoughts. He was a short man with blond hair and blue eyes, and I trusted him, certain he would help me. He volunteered to come to my apartment on a sunny Saturday afternoon where we could talk confidentially. (Using the word *gay* in public, like in a café or bar was risky because we might be overheard and exposed as gay.) Dr. R reassured me I was not gay because I was an attractive woman to him and to other men. He said he could show me something that would prove I wasn't gay and could cure me—just lick his penis, known today as a blow job. He pulled it out of his pants, but I had no idea what to do with it. I held this flaccid dick in my left hand and planted one small, dry kiss on top of it, having had zero experience in such matters. But he kept squirming around and moaning, "I can't get it up, I can't get it up! I'm so sorry, I don't know what's wrong."

At that point I stood up and directed him to leave. He zipped up his pants, humbly hung his head, and raced out of my living room. Such audacity that a professor would sexually abuse a student. He was known as a person in a position of trust who advocated for strict ethics between a counselor and a client. Such hypocrisy. I'm certain I was not the first or last woman who Dr. R violated.

Women have endured sexual assaults for thousands of years especially from men in power and even men from women's and girls' own families. If I had reported this abuse to the dean, would I fail the class? Would Dr. R refuse to recommend me for any future jobs? He avoided me for the rest of the semester and gave me an A in his class, which ironically included a full unit on the ethics of counseling. I bet every woman has several instances of sexual misconduct in her life. Mine started at age ten after ice skating. It's called male privilege, male power, and male supremacy. Let it end soon. Women are fed up.

When I told Judith what happened, she was disgusted: "You must do something!" But before sexual harassment laws were passed, the victim was, and often still is, disbelieved and becomes known as a troublemaker, which could seriously damage her career prospects. When I finally found the courage thirty years later to report Dr. R, which could revoke his state salary and pension, I found out he had died at age seventy. I had waited too long. Had I reported it, would I have faced a lawsuit, threats, and a possible backlash on me and my family? Now I personally understand why women don't "just speak up" as so many people believe a victim should do. It takes colossal courage; it is risky. Cheers for the thousands of women in the #MeToo movement who have spoken up.

CHAPTER 8

Graduate School and Growing an Activist Backbone

Meanwhile Judith and I continued to debate whether we were "that way" (gay) but were also too nervous to utter the word *gay* in public places. In the 1970s and centuries before us, LGBTQ people spoke in code so that no eavesdroppers could repeat hateful gossip about them and ruin their reputations, careers, or even kill them. Some examples of gay "code" were "We are that way," "We are family," "We are friends of Dorothy." But who in the world was Dorothy? It seems that Judy Garland, a singer and actress who played little Dorothy in the *Wizard of Oz* had become a beloved diva worshipped by thousands of gay men. I began thinking maybe I should not have married a man; if I'd known I was gay, I might have married a woman. How should I tell my husband I might have made a mistake? He would never understand.

Judith's and my first lesbian political action was attending the 1977 Houston, Texas, International Women's Conference, where we cheered Rep. Barbara Jordan, First Lady Barbara Bush, Rep. Bella Abzug, feminist writer Gloria Steinem, and little-known feminist musician Holly Near. At the conference we met hundreds of gay women who were doctors, lawyers, artists, teachers, entertainers, and social workers. They seemed like perfectly normal and accomplished women. I needed these role models to confirm that gays were not "sick." Judith and I even gathered up the courage to display gay political buttons. Mine read "I'm One Too" and Judith's, a lover of the outdoors, read "Mother Nature Is a Lesbian." A few other buttons seen at the conference included these feminist and gay gems: "We Try Harder and Get Paid Less," "Every Mother Is a Working Mother," "Don't Call Me Girl! God Created Woman in Her Own Likeness," "Give Us This Day Our Human Rights," "Older Women Do It Better," "Women Make Policy, Not Coffee," "Sexism Is a Social Disease," "ERA No Time Limit on Equality," "Praise the Goddess and Pass the Ammunition!"

"Coming out gay" could be frightening and even dangerous back then. For example, Judith wanted to hear this rising star vocalist Holly Near sing at a Denver lesbian dive bar called the Three Sisters. Since I was eight months pregnant at the time, Judith felt safe that being seen with a presumably heterosexual, pregnant woman would be confirmation that she was also heterosexual. Before entering the bar, however, Judith drove around and around the parking lot to see if she could identify any cars belonging to teachers, counselors, or school administrators who might be inside and would identify her as a lesbian. (Of course, what would they be doing in a gay bar?) Being gay could get you shamed and fired, and Judith had a whole career ahead of her, so I understood her healthy paranoia.

I was struggling with my own sexuality but by then I had a husband, a two-year-old daughter and an upcoming birth. I would have to make big decisions much later. Fortunately, Judith ignored my advice of just getting married and living happily ever after. Instead she lived a long honest life as a successful lesbian high school counselor, an Equal Rights Amendment (ERA) and Parents and Families of Lesbians and Gays (PFLAG) activist, and the founder of the Denver Sage Singers, an LGBTQ senior chorus.

When Don returned again from Vietnam, we needed to re-establish our marriage, and we were excited to be assigned to the Whidbey Island Naval Air Station (NAS) in Washington State, fifty miles north of Seattle.

Even with my new counseling degree, how could I possibly find a job on a remote Navy base? I remembered my dear mother Polly's advice: see where a need exists, prepare a method to address it, write a rationale and proposal for it, and discuss it with the decision-makers. I had heard that the community college on the mainland, Skagit Valley Community College (SVCC), was opening a branch on Whidbey Island. Surely this new branch would need a counselor. I prepared the written rationale and job proposal for such a branch, made an appointment with the director, and persuaded him to hire me as the branch's half-time counselor.

"Surely," I pleaded with Dr. Macomber, "all the officers and enlisted personnel will need career counseling as they retire and prepare for jobs in the civilian world." He finally agreed. Then one year later, the main branch of the SVCC in Mount Vernon, Washington, needed a full-time counselor. Suddenly, I had a full-time job, allowing us to begin to plan for Don's next career: medicine. Don had rejected aviation. "Flying as a commercial pilot is like being a glorified bus driver," he explained. "Not for me!" he said. As a career counselor, I'd encouraged Don to pursue a medical degree like his brother Norm. I even wrote his letter explaining why he wanted to be a doctor. But he needed prerequisites beyond his civil engineering degree. I insisted that he enroll at Western Washington State University in Bellingham while the GI Bill and my one income supported our family.

As someone who thought she knew everything (being from such cosmopolitan areas as Maine, Nebraska, and Colorado), I was shocked to meet and then counsel hundreds of SVCC students who were from a variety of disadvantaged upbringings and held multiple points of view about war, peace, patriotism, sexuality, guaranteed income, college debt, drugs, alcohol, marijuana, and environmental damage. Talk about diversity. This student body I was to counsel included survivalists, draft dodgers, conscientious objectors, gun owners, anti-war protesters, displaced homemakers, rape and incest victims, single mothers, fishermen, hunters, lumberjacks, artists, writers, and drug addicts—those we now call "non-traditional" students.

What did I know about these students' life experiences? How could I help them plan an education and a career? My work at SVCC taught me about the real-life achievement gaps and the income inequality gaps. Unlike them I had been blessed with not experiencing hunger and poverty or being raised in a broken home. I decided to learn from my fellow counselors their approaches to helping these students plan successful careers and lives.

Lessons I learned at SVCC: I will practice servant leadership, tied to my life's mission of "Something's wrong—Let's Fix It" for all of these students who are less fortunate than I am. Not to be a savior, but to help others seeking their American dream, as I was seeking mine. I particularly remember three young women. Renée wondered if the deer she shot, dressed, and froze would last through the winter or if she'd have to go ice fishing to feed her toddler. Claire lived with an alcoholic, abusive boyfriend just to ensure a roof over her head. Sandra gutted fish at the local cannery. When other counselors saw Sandra in my office they informed me, "Sandra has a very low IQ, can be suicidal, and can only be reached by playing physical games with her. She'll never be able to look you in the eye or converse with you." I decided to see if Sandra would venture out to play tennis or DONKEY with me.

After three weeks of playing DONKEY and some tennis with me, Sandra started secretly slipping her sorrowful poems under my office door. As we slowly discussed them, she began to hesitantly mention her grandfather. At the next week's reading of poems and discussion, Sandra stammered in a barely audible voice," My grandfather . . . touches . . . touches . . ." With tears in my eyes, I gently asked, "Will you go with me to see the friendly college psychologist?" No one had ever trained me to counsel victims of child sexual abuse and incest. I needed guidance from the psychologist. But Sandra frowned and said, "No psychologist . . . because . . . my grandfather will . . . will . . . beat me up . . . if he finds out."

To at least continue our trusting relationship, we kept playing tennis and discussing her poems; at one point she revealed to me that her favorite book was *Nobody Knows My Name*. Eventually she trusted me so much that she agreed to fly with me in the small Cessna 180 plane after I had earned my private pilot's license. Flying with her in sunny blue skies over the forested San Juan Islands and sparkly ocean waves was the first time I ever saw Sandra smile or laugh.

For the first time in twelve months, I felt heartsick to have to disconnect with Sandra because Don and I were moving to Omaha where he would attend the NU medical school. I still wonder what became of Sandra, Claire, and Renée. I advised each of them and others on how to attain their education and career goals, and I pray that they have reached them. I maintained a pen pal correspondence with Sandra for ten years, but after I mentioned in a Christmas letter that I was divorced and dating a gay woman, I never heard from her again. She had mentioned to me once that her minister had declared that homosexuality is a sin and an abomination.

Despite all the strife, violence, and unrest of the 1970s, I felt blessed with my Navy wife and college counselor experiences, but my shift from conservative to liberal and from timid to courageous made me more outspoken, a "difficult woman" as we were called then and a feminist activist.

After Don and I moved to Omaha for his medical training, I began to wonder how I would ever find a job as I did in Washington. I applied at Omaha Public Schools and noticed a counseling position at Omaha Northwest High School, a new structure built like Alcatraz—brick, steel, no windows, lots of fire extinguishers, and barbed wire around the school. This 1970s bomb-proof architecture needed to withstand grenades, acid, fire, bombs, and tear gas in case of revolts, protests, and violence. I interviewed for the job, citing my community college experience with a diversity of disadvantaged students and managing a community college's uprisings, protests, and even a bombing. I was hired.

Other than classrooms and counseling offices with no windows, the high school's interior was quite a different story from the barricaded exterior: lots of plants, trees, and fluorescent lighting, which created a sunny, humid, and warm climate. The school was bursting with award-winning teachers, high GPAs, and award-winning arts, theater, and sports programs. I sponsored the National Honor Society and the Hootenanny Club, as folk music and guitars were the entertainment of the day—no FM radio, no iPods or CDs. Think Kingston Trio; Peter, Paul and Mary; Joan Baez; Bob Dylan; Judy Collins, and John Denver. We listened to 45 rpm records and reel-to-reel tape recordings. Thanks to my dear mother who had given me a Framus golden wood folk guitar, I was able to teach myself exactly ten chords that covered practically every popular folk song of the day. I even dressed very "fashionably" like other educators and students with bell-bottom trousers, sandals, tie-dyed shirts with peace symbols, long hair, and beards. (No I didn't grow a beard.) While I was helping the students prepare for college entrance exams and applications, Don was graduating from the NU medical school and would soon start an internship in Greeley, Colorado.

But the absolute highlight of the early 1970s for me was the birth of my first daughter, a spunky six-pound, two-ounce-nineteen-inch Mary Catherine Schafer, whom her father called "the runt of the litter." She was the smallest of all the newborns lined up in the warmers, and I felt like a total failure for delivering such a tiny infant. But this tiny infant showed exceptionalism being born breach, legs coming out first instead of a head. "Does anyone see a head?" the doctor frantically asked. "I've got a leg, now someone find an arm; hurry up, here comes a shoulder; keep pulling; get the whole body and don't forget the head; is it still breathing; hey, we've got a girl!" Even in my dazed state, I knew that baby Mary would survive this breech birth because I had eaten super-healthy food like giant servings of bloody calf liver every night for the last eight months.

Thus our healthy baby had arrived, eyes flashing, sucking her thumb, sneezing, and greeting her audience with, "I'm here, world, get ready!" Although a control freak, I was shockingly helpless in childbirth. I had just read what humorist Erma Bombeck once quipped: "Having a baby can be a scream." Many screams. When the nurse from hell announced that she was going to "clean up your baby and then you're going to feed her," I cried, "No! Not yet! How do I feed a baby? I was never a babysitter!"

Nurse Ratchet sternly reminded me I had already toughened up my nipples, and Baby Jaws was hungry. In those days we mothers were instructed to toughen up our nipples by rubbing them vigorously with a terry cloth towel. Ouch! Also, a baby today in the breach position likely would precipitate a mandatory C-section now.

I was totally unprepared for motherhood. Three days later when my friend Ginny called to ask how Mary was, I asked, "Mary who?" Learning to become a mother to this tiny foreign object would take time. Gazing at her pink, little, wrinkled body, I wondered, *What in the world have I done?*

Soon I began to see examples of Mary's "I'm here, world, get ready" attitude: sitting in a grocery cart at age one and a half, smiling, waving, and greeting complete strangers with an enthusiastic "Hi!" or "Hug the baby!" Her huge head and tiny body also prompted shoppers to ask how this infant learned to say, "What's that?" which she often did because she was very curious.

At age two, Mary decided she could dive into the deep outdoor pool at Thompson Valley High School. She jumped in, waving at other swimmers, splashing and sputtering and began to sink as I raced over and barely caught her. Also at age two she started to announce to total strangers, "There's a baby sister in Mommy's uterus!" I had painstakingly used the correct reproductive terms when I informed her there may be a baby brother there, but she was adamant that it was a sister.

One frightening 1975 fall day in Omaha, young Mary knew something was wrong when we jerked around hearing a loud roll of thunder and piercing sirens signaling a tornado. Rushing to the basement, we cowered in the damp, cold cellar listening to what sounded like a Boeing 707 flying over at 500 feet. We were just thankful to survive, unlike some of our less fortunate neighbors.

Relieved and happy to leave the Nebraska tornadoes and medical school behind, our family moved to Greeley, Colorado, in 1976 where Don entered a family practice residency. The other happy news was the birth of a second beautiful daughter, Ann Elizabeth Schafer, at seven pounds, twelve ounces, and twenty-one inches long, and known as a "Centennial Baby" because Colorado Statehood had been won in 1876 one hundred years earlier. Annie came into this world under a golden harvest moon soon after we'd gathered pumpkins, squash, and tomatoes from our garden. Rushing to the hospital at eleven p.m., I was placed on a waiting list in a chilly, dark corridor for women in labor. I was number ten and the delivery room was full. When my turn finally came, soon upon entering the delivery room, a slippery, slimy infant burst out of me and was caught by the night nurse who cracked that Annie was her "catch of the day." All I could gasp was a feeble, "Good catch, thank you."

Unlike her sister Mary, at the moment of birth, Annie smiled sweetly, blinked her eyes, and rested her head gently on my belly. One doctor stated he'd never delivered such a peaceful newborn, one who seemed to have no worries. I realized that Annie was fresh from God when I admired her one-quarter-inch, perfectly formed fingernails. She'll obviously become a concert pianist, I thought. Well, that didn't happen. Seamstress, wife, mother, master chef, and banker are good enough.

Upon Annie's arrival at home, two-year-old Mary looked her over, squinted into her mouth, and shrieked, "Where are her teeth? Mommy, she doesn't have any teeth!" I reassured Mary that Annie's teeth would come soon. These two girls became BFFs (best forever friends) as long as Annie obeyed every one of bossy Mary's commands. My favorite memory with both babies is the two-a.m. rocking-chair feedings of a soft, slumbering infant, sucking and slurping. I can still smell the creamy, rose fragrance on their silky skin. In reverie and awe, I felt like I had become the Earth Mother, the mother of all creation.

Annie's arrival was a special joy after so much grief caused by the Colorado Big Thompson River flood on July 31, 1976, which killed 157 people. Tourists and motorists were caught in a raging river sweeping down a narrow, curving highway with jagged boulders

Something's Wrong. Let's Fix It.

on both sides. Cars crashed into the sides, thrusting occupants onto the rocks or downstream into punishing currents. Victims had been advised to stay in their vehicles, which was wrong; had they been told to leave their car and climb to safety, many lives would have been saved. Thus today as you drive along Highway 34 west to Estes Park, you see frequent signs: CLIMB TO SAFETY.

As a mother in the 1970s I was advised to keep track of sweet and humorous things our children said. *Kids Say the Darnedest Things* was a best-selling book by comedian Art Linkletter, so I scribbled notes on food-splattered paper and slapped them on the refrigerator door. I suppose today in 2024 mothers put these comments in their cell phones or in their computers. Here are some of my daughters' 1970s classics from ages two to five:

Annie (with a cold) to Mom: "Help! My nose came undone."

Annie to friends (when toddlers said where their mothers work, e.g., Coors, Hewlett Packard, and Loveland Hospital): "My mother works for the ERA." (Equal Rights Amendment)

Teacher to Mary: "What nice cowboy boots you have, Mary." Mary replied, "These are not cowboy boots, these are cowgirl boots!"

Mary to Mom: "The women are going to sneak up on the men to get the ERA, aren't they?!"

Mom reading a book to Mary: "Are Quil and Zay men or women?" Mary: "Probably men." Mom: "Why?" Mary: "Because most people in stories are men." (Ouch)

Mom to Annie: "How'd you get so darn cute?" Annie: "I just came that way."

Meanwhile, Annie soon developed the backbone to challenge Mary's commands: "I will not ride in your dump truck, I will not drink this milk, and I will not fetch your doll." Annie later exhibited her youthful cooking skills when the girls accidentally locked the door of the self-cleaning oven while a gingerbread was baking. Luckily, no flames burst out and we were able to force open the door with screwdrivers. Henceforth, the Schafer girls' crusty Gingerbread Brûlée with whipped cream is a family favorite.

I noticed Annie was fascinated with fashion and jewelry when unbeknownst to me she took my $5,000 diamond ring to preschool. (Why was I so careless with this valuable piece of jewelry?) She later explained she wanted her doll to have something "pretty." When I noticed it was missing, I panicked and called the director and asked if she'd seen a large diamond ring. "Yes," she explained. "It's right here in the toy box and we are lucky we found it. Annie wanted her Madame Alexander doll to have a diamond." Thankfully I recovered it. As a new mother I learned: Do not leave things of great value within a child's reach.

I was thankful my girls were pretty much no-nonsense children and rarely got upset about anything, but they always reprimanded me when I consistently missed the turn into our beloved Wendy's where we hungry ladies devoured greasy cheeseburgers, crispy French fries, and thick chocolate Frosties.

Determined to expose the girls to numerous activities, I introduced them to swimming, ice skating, skiing, trampolining, cheerleading, jogging, cat care, and traveling. I encouraged them to try water skiing with legendary Evergreen High School volleyball coach and friend, Lo Hunter, who piloted her speedboat over placid Lake Loveland. I took the girls to learn ice skating at the EPIC Skating/Hockey Center in Fort Collins and dressed them in frilly pink tutus as they glided around the arena and even learned to jump and skate backward. One passion we had was attending the Denver Ice Capades featuring heartthrobs like Brian Boitano in his silvery spandex tights.

Our annual summer trips to Cape Cod with the Spilman family were our most treasured vacations. There we spent our days collecting shells, catching hermit crabs, melting butter to slather on lobster and corn on the cob, and licking jamoca almond fudge ice cream at Friendly's, the East Coast's favorite ice cream shoppe. The girls' dad made sure they learned to ski the black-diamond slopes of Colorado while I engaged them in the arts by taking them to *The Music Man, La Cage aux Folles, ET*, and a throbbing Neil Diamond concert at the Denver Pepsi Center.

CHAPTER 9

Troubled Waters

In addition to raising two lively daughters in Greeley, this area turned out to be the turning point in my life. But first my nose told me that I was in Greeley, Colorado, because of the pungent manure odor which locals called the "smell of money" and which wafted in the city from feedlots and slaughterhouses. In Greeley I entered the doctoral education program at the University of Northern Colorado (UNC). With gratitude to my blessed mother, Grandma Polly often babysat, cooked, and cleaned for me while I attended classes during the day and studied late into the night after my daughters went to bed. Reading textbooks and journals before the age of computers meant enduring long waits at the library for needed documents, books, and journals to be returned. And typing a dissertation before word processors required using the slippery "self-erasing" paper that smeared black ink on one's hands, and then having to hire a highly paid professional typist to complete the manuscript error-free. But what could my dissertation topic possibly be?

Researching any dissertation topic required me to find an original "burning issue" to study and conduct research related to the topic. Feeling sorry for myself, I wondered what would engage me enough to spend hours poring over journals in the library? To make matters worse, most journals were available only on interlibrary loan, so it could take weeks to acquire specific articles. What topic could possibly excite and sustain me for this endurance test? I refused to end up in the wasteland of ABD (All But Dissertation), which applies to graduate students who passed all the classes but failed to complete the marathon dissertation.

Fortunately, my elderly adviser who looked and sounded like John Dewey had heard about a new 1972 federal civil rights law called Title IX of the Educational Amendments of 1972. This Title IX prohibited discrimination based on sex in schools and colleges that received federal financial assistance. "Would you be interested in that?" he asked. "Of course, I would," I stammered, and then wondered if the law would possibly apply to girls and women having access to high school and college athletics. Would this Title IX be the "fix it" I'd wanted for over twenty years that would allow girls like me to play and compete in sports? Wow, finally there is hope!

Finally, I had found my dissertation topic: I would teach a class to thirty-five teachers in the Greeley Public Schools about sex discrimination in K–12 education, testing their knowledge in a pretest, and then again checking their knowledge in a posttest. Results? These teachers showed significant improvement in knowing how to stop sexist behaviors and they could not believe their behaviors were sexist because they believed they treated boys and girls exactly the same! These unconscious sexist behaviors included calling on boys more often than girls; asking boys higher-level questions; standing closer to boys and smiling more at boys; channeling girls into secretarial, teaching, and nursing jobs instead of a broad choice of careers; excluding girls from interscholastic sports; asking only boys to run the AV equipment; hiring only men for school principal and superintendent jobs; and omitting the study of women's contributions to history, art, science, and literature.

One of the worst of these behaviors was telling millions of girls over the centuries that they were no good at math. Today, however, in 2023 high school girls are scoring very near boys on state mathematics assessments. I would love to observe some classrooms today in 2024 and determine if these sexist behaviors have stopped. None of my sex discrimination teaching in the Greeley public schools would have been possible without the support and enthusiasm of Dr. Ron Hildebrand, the director of staff development, who arranged for the teachers to receive three credit hours toward recertification of their teaching licenses. I thankfully had met a visionary, open-minded, and progressive man.

One way I kept my dissertation in perspective and did not think it was the greatest one ever written in humankind was when I saw a dumpster near my UNC adviser's office. When I asked him what was in the dumpster he said, "Just thirty hard-bound dissertations—they're headed for the recycle." You spend hours, days, months, and years on this document, and it lands in the recycle? I guess my dissertation did not change the world; maybe it did make things better if other school districts learned about non-sexist teaching and offered such a class to their teachers. Those teachers would likely improve their instruction to be fair to both girls and boys. Unfortunately I've heard in the business world that bosses often call on men more than women, stand closer to men, and ask men higher-level questions. I will check out Sheryl Sandberg's book *Lean In: Women, Work, and the Will to Lead*. I'm sure there are other books about how women can get ahead in the country and world.

Upon completing my doctoral classes and defending my dissertation, *A Description of an Inservice Workshop for Raising Teachers'*

Awareness of Sex Discrimination in Education (1979), I was thrilled to not be an ABD, but an Ed.D. (Doctor of Education), and was ready for my next career as an administrator in a school district, university, or agency.

During a celebratory happy hour that we called a Friday Afternoon Club (FAC), my graduate colleagues and our professors gathered at a local cantina to celebrate our accomplishments. In the middle of balloons, crepe paper, margaritas, and nachos, however, I felt someone's warm, scratchy hand slide quickly up under my skirt along my inner thigh reaching for my private parts. I jumped up and screamed, "Stop it! What are you doing?" My graduate school adviser sitting next to me thought it was his prerogative to violate his ethics and take advantage of a vulnerable woman who'd just reached the high mark in her career. Again, like the previous professor at CU-Boulder who had exposed himself to me, this UNC professor, Dr. N took advantage of me.

Again, a person in a position of trust abused a subordinate. After reading my dissertation about sexist behavior, he apparently believed it didn't apply to him, that he was above the law. He exercised his white male power over me—I assumed I was not the first or last of his abuses.

I'm angry and frustrated that for many centuries, women have been victims of sexual predators who hold high ranks and power over them. And it continues. One of the worst cases was that of the US film producer and convicted sex offender Harvey Weinstein, who for thirty years raped and required sex from eighty young women auditioning for movie roles. His abuses sparked the #MeToo social media campaign when thousands of women told their stories of being violated. Victimization of girls and women continues to this day in 2024. As the mother of two daughters and three young granddaughters, I pray that this behavior will stop, but I have little confidence that it will.

During and after the social and political upheaval in the 1960s and '70s, I was surprised to hear our UNC professors claim that public education's traditional purpose had been to perpetuate the white male status quo, but that education's new mission was to prepare students of all races, ethnicities, genders, religions, languages, and disabilities for successful futures. Prior to the Civil Rights Act of 1964, Title IX in 1972, and the Education for All Handicapped Children Act (Public Law 94–142) in 1975, public schools and colleges had provided many advantages for able-bodied white boys and men. But this new approach about discrimination in education and society only confirmed my early high school determination that "something's wrong—let's fix it."

When I learned in graduate school about the limited opportunities for students who were African American, Hispanic, Indigenous, LGBTQ, limited English proficient, and disabled, I realized the huge challenges that lay ahead. The new laws and also my professors demanded that my fellow students and I take responsibility for correcting the wrongs against these groups of pupils, all historically denied equal rights. But how could I fix such massive systemic discrimination? Certainly not by myself.

Graduating from UNC in 1979 at the age of thirty-seven as a young mother with a doctorate in education, I had become an academic feminist, researcher, scholar, and political activist. The knowledge I'd gained from the CU-Boulder civil rights movement and the UNC graduate program, however, began to cause me high anxiety. It was clear—huge social and personal change was ahead. Even in the conservative city of Greeley, the National Organization for Women (NOW) had formed a chapter. I said to myself, *I'm not interested in meeting a bunch of weed-smoking hippies from Haight-*

Asbury, hairy naked radicals from Woodstock, or burn-the-bra lesbians from Greenwich Village. Should I sneak into a NOW meeting, just to confirm my suspicions?

I was so wrong. There I met lawyers, teachers, homemakers, dog groomers, city planners, and state senators, mostly straight women but a few gay women. These women were laser-focused on passing the Equal Rights Amendment (ERA). The ERA states that "Equality of rights under the law shall not be denied or abridged by the United States or by any state on account of sex." Women are not included in the US Constitution except when they won the 19th Amendment, which was the right to vote in 1920. There is still no legal protection in the US Constitution guaranteeing women protection under the law.

Laws passed by Congress and states explain why there is equal pay for equal work, sexual harassment and rape are now illegal, and women can get credit in their own name. Despite the passage of these civil rights laws, the truth is that these laws are not self-enforcing, and unless someone or some group files grievances through the courts, these laws are broken without any consequences. Thankfully, law-abiding citizens, corporations, schools, businesses, and legislatures willingly now obey these laws. NOW members provided crucial services such as securing attorneys to prosecute offenders, sending letters to the editor, recruiting pro-women candidates to run for offices, raising money for them, working to get them elected, contacting and lobbying elected officials, and staging demonstrations.

I decided to become active with NOW so my two small daughters would have opportunities I never had. Landmark laws and organizations charged with providing assistance to anyone breaking a law or a person who is the victim of a broken law include but are not limited to the Civil Rights Law of 1964, Equal Employment Opportunity Commission, and the Office for Civil Rights.

True to activist form, Greeley NOW and I planned to protest sex discrimination in Denver at a women's rights rally at the federal building with Representative Pat Schroeder (D-Denver) in 1979. Staring and pointing at me, Greeley NOW members asked, "Can anyone play guitar and lead a song at the courthouse?" Okay, I agreed to do it and brought my five-year-old daughter, Mary, with me. We activists used guitars and protest songs as powerful media for expressing rage at forms of oppression. Bob Dylan's "The Times They Are A-Changing" and Helen Reddy's "I Am Woman" blasted the air waves at rallies, protests, and marches. I practiced and performed songs like "We Shall Overcome" with the protesters who wore their No More War, Era Yes, and "59¢" T-shirts. (Fifty-nine cents is what women were paid compared to one dollar for men in the 1970s. Today in 2023 the ratio is eighty-two cents for women compared to one dollar for men according to the Pew Research Center. Not much progress. After the Denver rally, back home in Loveland, future feminist daughter Mary proudly bragged to fellow kindergarteners that "Mommy sang for the President of the United States." Not quite.

At the NOW meetings and socials, I met gay professional women who belied the stereotype of hairy, scary lesbians with key chains, plaid shirts, and short butch hair. Hoping to avoid and reject my growing attraction to women, I knew I had to decide: Am I straight or gay? I had learned from the Greeley and Colorado NOW meetings that there are thousands of smart, courageous, and professional gay and straight women. After moving to Loveland, I found myself torn with looming decisions: Do I stay married to a good man as we raise our daughters and look like the happy American family? Do I stay married and maybe become a school board member or PTA leader? Or do Don and I separate, I find a good job, and he and I share joint custody of our beloved daughters? All options were unthinkable.

Terrified to admit to my husband my growing attraction to women, I immersed myself in founding the Loveland, Colorado, NOW chapter. It grew to fifty activists, even in a conservative small town, and led me to the Denver and Colorado chapters of NOW to learn state and national politics—first as president of Loveland NOW and later as secretary of Colorado NOW. A hidden agenda was for me to meet more gay women in order to help me decide my sexual orientation. I'd had attractions to girls and women since the age of thirteen, including a serious crush on singer and actress Judy Garland. But in the heterosexual zeitgeist of high school, college, and young teacher FACs (Friday Afternoon Clubs), I'd never met one gay woman, or so I thought. *What exactly is a lesbian?* I wondered. Even my wise Kappa sisters kept reassuring me that I'd soon learn to love men sexually. I was uncertain about that.

For example, one sorority sister advised me to simply open my mouth wide when a man wanted to kiss me; how can you kiss with your mouth wide open? A Beta Theta Pi man I dated briefly wanted me to rub his genital area, but it was wet; why had he wet his pants? So naïve. Not until I enjoyed a few flings with gay women in Denver did I experience physical and sexual gratification. I knew these flings were wrong and unfaithful to my husband whom I loved. But in my young, sheltered life there were no *Our Bodies Ourselves* or *Loving Women* books to educate us about the female body and sexuality.

Here is what sex education at Lincoln High School in the late 1950s looked like: "Listen up, girls and boys: girls, go to room 205; boys, go to room 306. Close all those doors and pull down the shades." There we viewed films about female and male body parts. Girls learned about menstruation and pregnancy, and boys learned about ejaculation and the evils of masturbation.

Feeling ashamed and terrified of telling my husband about these sexual flings after Colorado NOW meetings, I prepared to tell him the truth sometime. But an angry lesbian in Denver NOW, whose amorous advances I had rejected, telephoned him one night and asked, " How do you like it that your wife is out dancing at a gay bar? Don't you know that your wife is gay?"

When I returned that night, he angrily confronted me with this information, which I promptly denied. He said: "Now I know what was really going on after the NOW meetings and that you were cheating on me! I want a divorce. I thought we were husband and wife for life!"

I said I was just having fun at a women's bar after the NOW meeting, but of course this was a lie.

One month later I gathered the courage to admit to him that I must be gay, but I didn't know it when I married him. I was certain I would learn to love him as all my friends had promised me. I apologized for causing him this pain because he was a loving, protective husband and father. And I did love him as the brother I had always wanted. He deserved a better life with a heterosexual woman, while I would seek to live a life of integrity and authenticity as a single, gay mother. But this prospect for me was very daunting.

Most important of all was the welfare of our six- and four-year-old daughters, Mary and Annie. As frightening as a separation or divorce appeared, I first believed we must stay together "for the good of the children." But he and I decided a divorce would be necessary for each of us to have fulfilling lives. I feared that our beloved little daughters would be devastated and damaged for life. When and how would we ever tell them?

After the decision to get divorced, I worried about how I could support myself—where would I find a good job, where would I live, how would I get joint custody of my daughters, and how or will my sister and friends help me in this new situation? Getting divorced was difficult, and I was embarrassed to reveal this to my sister and friends; they might be so surprised and worried. My best friend, Judith, however, understood all the problems I would face and how she would help me. I had revealed my anxieties about being a single lesbian mother to my sister and to several friends who thankfully all offered their support. Several of them even said they were not surprised because I did not seem happy with my husband and marriage.

Fortunately, I had just started working in Denver at the Colorado Department of Education (CDE) and could support myself with a decent salary, rent a Loveland duplex, and vanpool to Denver. To avoid more disruption for the girls, Don and I decided that keeping them in our family home was best, with his hiring a person to assist with childcare, meals, laundry, and housework. I would live at my nearby duplex, spending every Wednesday night with our daughters, and we would trade off on weekends. His transition was made easier when he soon met a loving registered nurse to date and marry.

CHAPTER 10

Mission Accomplished with Title IX

Leaving the security of married life and spending less time with my precious daughters was not as rational a decision as I had anticipated. The girls cried when we told them that we were divorcing. "Can't we just be a normal family again? Can't you just work things out?" they pleaded. My journals at that time reflect my tears, despair, and heartache. Could I really support myself and live an honest life as a single gay mother? Would my girls miss their mother and feel abandoned? Probably. Would they hold this against her for the rest of their lives? Possibly. Would their father attempt to obtain sole custody of the girls? Yes. Would he distort the truth about what happened, i.e., "Sue deserted her children and ran off to Denver to become a lesbian"? Yes, these were his exact words according to my friends who heard them often. Would he threaten to expose me as a lesbian to my employer and my community? Yes.

I would often stand over the girls' beds, crying and wondering if I'd done a selfish thing, fearful that he'd move out of state, and I'd never see them again.

Especially painful for me was his early and constant demand for sole custody. I quickly realized I needed a lawyer. Our joint custody compromise was eventually facilitated by a feminist attorney who was thrilled to litigate the first lesbian joint custody case in Colorado. "Gays and lesbians are unfit parents," ignorant ministers, priests, and doctors proclaimed. The prospect of this case being splashed across local, state, and national media was suddenly embarrassing enough for my husband to quickly agree to joint custody and finally to a fair financial settlement. I had read a book titled *How to Divorce Your Wife*, which warned women of what tactics angry husbands would use, like trying to take all the assets instead of a fair fifty-fifty amount. Also, I had paid for his and my living expenses during both his post-graduate and medical school years, worth two million dollars over his lifetime, which I decided not to pursue.

But coming out for any gay person in the 1980s was dangerous. Fear of being fired, bullied, harassed, killed, disinherited, ridiculed, or rejected by family and friends was the new reality. Many ministers preached that gays were immoral, and some psychologists pronounced that gays were sick and that homosexuality was a disease. However, without much publicity, the American Psychological Association (APA) in 1972 removed homosexuality from its list of illnesses, finding that most gays, like most straights, are capable, ethical, healthy, and law-abiding citizens. I knew that!

Some communities of faith today still cling to their disdain of LGBTQs by declaring that they "hate the sin but love the sinner." How can I be a sinner if I am a loving mother, partner, sister, friend, neighbor, educator, and law-abiding citizen? And aren't we all God's children? Galatians 3:28 says, "There is no longer slave or free; there is no longer male and female, for all of you are one in Christ Jesus." *All* means all with no exceptions as I interpret the Bible.

For centuries the hatred and subjugation of gays and lesbians caused the loss of many great scientific, literary, and artistic talents. From studying LGBTQ history and literature, I knew that thousands of gays nevertheless lived and thrived incognito as painters in the French caves of Lascaux, Michelangelo, Joan of Arc, Gertrude Stein, and Willa Cather to name a few. Gays died in gas chambers in Nazi Germany. In efforts to pass for straight, many gay people suffered from drug and alcohol addictions. I wonder how many men died of HIV/AIDS due to unprotected sex but also to fear and hatred from the general public? As of 2018 about 700,000 people in the US have died of HIV/AIDS and about 13,000 per year. But after centuries of hate and discrimination, the June 28, 1969, Stonewall Inn Gay Bar uprising in New York City set in motion newfound activism. (The Stonewall Bar is now a National Monument.) Federal Equal Employment Opportunity (EEO) laws eventually followed, prohibiting discrimination based on sexual orientation. Growing social acceptance, religious tolerance, and new research confirmed that homosexuals are as normal as heterosexuals. Gay men back then were labeled as pedophiles, but in fact we know now that sex crimes against children are mainly perpetrated by sick heterosexual men who know minors in the family. Gay women were seen as obese, unattractive jocks who couldn't attract a man. Today there are millions of healthy looking and attractive gay women who look just like healthy looking and attractive straight women.

As rocky as the joint custody situation became early on for our little girls, my worst fears for their well-being were not actualized. A counselor helped them deal with their sadness, anger, and fear. For myself, I sought legal and psychological help. Being a newly "out" single gay mother was, however, more challenging than I'd anticipated.

A psychologist helped me to manage my life, but unfortunately we became intimate partners, in violation of therapist-patient ethics.

Our relationship lasted nine years, and we did share many good times, like taking the girls water skiing, digging for hermit crabs in the Cape Cod tides, and visiting Smith College and the Statue of Liberty. She and I as partners encountered unexpected conflicts, however. My extrovert personality and her introvert one clashed. Always a social butterfly and political activist, I couldn't convince her to join in the political and feminist activism that inspired me, nor could she convince me to lead a quiet, peaceful life of bird watching, hiking, and reading. I was a victim of an unethical therapist who later lost her Colorado license.

Little did I know how much my teenage determination of "something's wrong—let's fix it" would also become my mission in life as an adult. Where did I get the audacity and courage to think that a little kid like me had the power to change this wrong and discriminatory system of excluding girls and women from sports, only later to be vindicated by the passage of Title IX in 1972? This law requires schools and colleges to offer athletics to both girls and boys, women and men. I remembered that the Bible declared, "All things are possible through God." And I still believe it. Apparently millions of parents and citizens across the country also believed that females should have access to sports, occupations, businesses, nonprofits, and elected positions.

I had only the highest expectations for the new Title IX law which prohibits gender discrimination in all publicly funded schools and colleges in employment, salaries, athletics, scholarships, housing, transportations, facilities, and publicity—exactly what I had demanded of my high school principal Mr. Bogar way back in 1958. The exact text of Title IX of the Educational Amendments of 1972 is: *No person in the United States shall on the basis of sex, be excluded from participation in, be denied the benefits of, or be subjected to discrimination under any educational program or activity receiving federal financial assistance.* Today in 2024 there is debate over whether trans girls and women are covered under Title IX. I believe that Title IX prohibits discrimination on the basis of sex, not on the basis of gender identity. But we will see what the US Office for Civil Rights declares about this and what US courts might decide about it.

I felt vindicated by helping to change a discriminatory practice that spanned hundreds of years of athletic competition in the United States. But passing the Title IX legislation was no easy task. Opposed by conservatives like the John Birch Society and the Eagle Forum, passage required strong leadership by Sen. Birch Bayh (D-IN), Rep. Patsy Mink (R-HI), Sen. Ted Kennedy (D-MA), the National Organization for Women (NOW), the Women's Sports Foundation (WSF), the National Association for the Advancement of Colored People (NAACP), the US Olympic Committee (USOC), and many more.

In my new job at the Colorado Department of Education (CDE), I was appointed as a civil rights consultant while training Colorado educators on the requirements of Title IX and the Civil Rights Act, as well as how to file a grievance with the Office for Civil Rights if Title IX or other laws were broken. I was blessed to be supervised by a fifty-year-old, dynamic African American woman named JRG, also known as Jay. She was my supervisor in the civil rights office. Jay had a hearty laugh, long red fingernails, and wore large gold earrings, five-inch heels, and bright-red dresses. Her office smelled like fresh-brewed coffee where we sipped and plotted how women would rule the world.

Jay decided she should expose this naïve white girl to African American culture, so she said, "Get dressed up—we're going to rocking, stomping Black gospel churches, Black cafés like M and D's

Bar BQ, and Pierre's Supper Club—all in the historic Denver African American neighborhood known as Five Points!" Then she dragged me to a conference of the Black Women for Political Action with over two hundred "sisters" wearing large, feathered hats, gold dangling jewelry, and gold high heels crying "Equal Rights Now!" I was the only white person in this sea of Black. I felt out of place, nervous, and uneasy, probably like many Blacks feel today when they attend majority-white events. Jay secured thousands of state and federal dollars for me so I could organize Title IX orientation conferences around the state. She even booked US Olympic Gold Medalist Jackie Joyner to speak at one of the conferences at Copper Mountain.

Jay also assigned me to drive Jackie over Loveland Pass (12,000 ft.) to deliver a speech called "Aim High, Win, and Thrive!" I looked forward to having two hours in the car with Jackie to pick her brain about achieving equality for female athletes even at the Olympic level. But she'd never been over a high mountain pass and became so frightened she couldn't even look out at the spacious green valleys and the snow-capped peaks. Being from St. Louis at sea level, it was understandable that Jackie suffered a bit of altitude sickness. But that never stops a champion, and she was able to fire up all 250 coaches with her message of setting high goals, persevering, and accomplishing them.

These accomplishments in Colorado would not have happened without the advocacy from the assistant commissioner of education, Mr. Roy Brubacher. Roy advised me on how to explain the requirements of Title IX to wary, disgruntled superintendents without being run out of town, especially in the 150 rural school districts. Roy was a sixty-year-old, short, stocky educator who wore black western boots, a white western shirt with fake pearl buttons, beige polyester pants held up by a belt with a cactus-shaped buckle, and a shiny navy sport coat. This gruff cowboy with the silver crew cut puffed on Marlboros all day in his fifth-floor corner office when state agencies prior to 1984 allowed smoking on-site.

Although Roy hardly resembled an advocate for such a feminist cause as Title IX, no one was more enthusiastic for it. And he didn't even have a daughter—just a sense of what is right and just for girls in Colorado. He approved every budget request my supervisor Jay and I submitted for conferences on how to implement sports for girls and women. He appointed me to represent the Colorado Department of Education on what he derisively called "that old boys' club," the Executive Board of the Colorado High School Activities Association (CHSAA). "That group needs diversity," said Roy, and I was proud to become the first woman ever appointed to this august position since CHSAA's formation in 1927.

The signs of our high, powerful status were the baby-blue, men's cut blazers with the CHSAA logo that we were required to wear to meetings and athletic contests. Since the manufacturer of the blazers didn't produce women's cuts, mine was so baggy and lumpy that fans and friends chuckled as they issued me "fashion citations." So, a woman rises to power only to look like a clown. Good thing I had a sense of humor.

Implementation of the letter and spirit of Title IX by the 1975 deadline continued to raise objections from school administrators. "This law is a half-baked idea that cannot work," the majority of male athletic directors and coaches cried early on across the state and nation. "This law will hurt our boys' egos. Girls aren't strong enough for competition; if they sweat, they'll become unfeminine. We have only one gym—and it's the boys' gym! We don't have the money, coaches, or officials to support girls' sports. We don't even have enough girls interested in participating." On and on went the excuses. But then, thousands of fathers, grandfathers, and uncles of current and future female athletes spoke out.

Many courageous women coaches and physical education teachers proposed workable strategies to accomplish both the letter and the spirit of Title IX. I say "courageous" women because many of the single women at that time risked being called lesbians if they advocated for women's equality in sports or society. Those wanting to maintain the status quo believed that accusing women of being gay would scare all the advocates away. It didn't work. Unfairly or not, I could avoid homophobic gossip by taking advantage of heterosexual privilege, having been married and the mother of two children. But I refused to use marital status whenever possible. Whatever it took, we convinced the good old boys that Title IX was not only the law of the land—it was also the right thing to do.

Many female leaders from groups such as those mentioned above stood tall at the microphones, and now fifty years later, there are 3.4 million high school girls participating in sports, compared to 30,000 in 1975. NCAA data in 2021 indicated there were 494,000 women participating in 10,586 collegiate championship sports while men compete in 9,159. Sports for girls and women now extend from the youth level to the international Olympics. Title IX also launched the adult and family fitness boom starting in the 1980s when former female athletes married their spouses, had children, and determined to make health and fitness a family priority. Corporations started marketing to women, and earned billions of dollars from sales of clothing, shoes, gear, and equipment for children and adults. Who knew that Title IX would be so good for business?

I thrived in my new job as the Title IX director at the CDE, traversing the mountains and prairies, offering workshops on sex bias in schools and how to provide sports for girls, all the while facing some hostile male athletic directors and principals. One prominent athletic director (AD) sporting a crew cut, baby-blue polyester pants, and white buck shoes (the 1980s AD uniform), pointed out to me the "boys' track" and sheepishly explained there could be NO girls' track and field because there's only one track. I innocently asked if the girls could possibly share the track with the boys. Grudgingly he acknowledged, "Yeah, the darn feds will make us do this."

When I asked, however, whether his own daughters wanted to compete, suddenly his attitude changed. Solution: Girls' and boys' schedules will enable both to use the track. Now, was that so difficult? Other athletic directors mentioned they were worried that girls would upstage boys and hurt the boys' egos. In schools, colleges, and even in the US Olympics, men and boys needed to learn how to share gyms, swimming pools, baseball/softball diamonds, tracks, ice rinks, and tennis courts. It seems simple today, but it's taken fifty years of activism, lawsuits, and eternal vigilance for the letter and spirit of Title IX to be achieved but never guaranteed. Threats against Title IX and equity for females are still ongoing, with myths like "Title IX destroyed men's gymnastics and wrestling" still circulating. This is incorrect. Those colleges or schools had decided not to fund these sports in their budgets that now must be divided approximately 50 percent male, 50 percent female. Do schools and colleges need ninety boys on their football teams? No. Those teams are eating up too much of the school's resources. If the schools reduced football they would be able to fund wrestling and/or gymnastics.

During these years at CDE, I was also learning how to "come out" as gay in my work and in my community. I had to be careful about what I said, where I had been, and with whom I had socialized. I felt guilty for "passing for straight" like keeping photos of my daughters prominently displayed on my office desk. I could not be seen at a grocery store or theater with my gay partner. I couldn't say what I was doing for the weekend like going dancing at a gay bar or to Aspen with the gay ski club. I was careful around my daughters' friends and their parents not to "look gay" or to mention my partner at their school events. I wasn't even sure what "looking gay" was, but I always had to think it through. It was even risky to say how fabulous the Denver Women's Chorus performance was. Would someone think this is really a lesbian chorus? In other words I was consumed with fear and paranoia, which was hardly a healthy way to live.

Today in 2024, LGBTQ people are still cautious with revealing their sexuality in certain situations and with certain people. On a recent trip to South America, my partner Barb and I decided when fellow tourists asked if we were sisters, I would say, "No, we are gay partners." Several of them said, "Great!" Others said, "We knew that." So the LGBTQ movement is making progress especially when the US Supreme Court voted in favor of gay marriage in 2015. Even Pope Francis in 2023 blessed gay partners but not gay marriage. Today trans women are at great risk for coming out, and in 2023 over twenty-five trans women were murdered in the US. Sad to say I am still careful with whom and where I share this personal information.

Still at CDE while working to implement Title IX, I worked to recruit one of the earliest energizers and motivational speakers for Title IX in Colorado, Lo Hunter. Lo Hunter was one of the most highly respected and winningest volleyball coaches in Colorado. At Evergreen High School, Lo guided her team to eight state championships, a record that's never been surpassed. A dainty but tough Kansas native, Lo had short, curly brown hair and wore tight bell-bottom pants, five-inch high heels, and one-inch long, diamond-studded fingernails to every competition. Her scratchy voice could be heard throughout the entire Evergreen two-court gymnasiums, which are now named for her.

An outspoken and respected leader, she volunteered long hours to instructing novice coaches in this "sissy" game, as volleyball was derisively called in the US, where many athletic directors and coaches had never heard of it. Soon, however, volleyball became a fierce, competitive sport for girls and women at the high school, NCAA, and international Olympic levels thanks to the sport's American pioneers like Lo Hunter. And recently in 2019, the CHSAA sanctioned high school boys' volleyball. Not such a sissy sport apparently.

The value of a mentor is priceless, and I owe any success I've had in my career to mentors like Jay, Roy, and Cookie, the associate athletic director in the Jefferson County School District, one of the largest in Colorado. I sought out Cookie for all kinds of advice regarding sports for girls and women. Cookie is an attractive blond woman standing five foot six who'd been a physical education teacher and gymnastics coach before becoming an athletic director. She speaks with a soft Southern drawl that belies the fire in her belly and in her heart.

In college she was a member of the world-renowned women's basketball team known as the Flying Queens from Texas Wayland Baptist University. Back in the 1950s and '60s, the NCAA didn't sponsor women's collegiate contests, but it was legal for a generous Texas pilot to fly the award-winning women (the Queens) around the country and world in his airplane. This competition was under the auspices of the AAU, the Amateur Athletic Union. Then in 1971, a group of women's sports professors and physical educators convened the AIAW (Association for Intercollegiate Athletics for Women), which sponsored collegiate competitions until 1981 when the NCAA, sensing prestige and profit, became the sponsor of US women's college athletics.

I noticed how Cookie could use her Southern charm and pleasing personality to tactfully man-handle hesitant male school administrators who had little sympathy for girls and women's sports. Cookie led many difficult battles within the Colorado High School Activities Association to sanction more sports for girls like volleyball, softball, and soccer while maintaining the traditional "female" sports like gymnastics, track and field, and tennis. Using lobbying techniques like personal phone calls and handwritten notes, Cookie utilized unfailing persistence with the good old boys who opposed more girls' sports because "they cost too much." Cookie would innocently ask, "Why do boys sports take 100 %t of a district's athletic budget now that we operate under Title IX when the athletic budget should be approximately 50% boys,50% girls?" The men had no answer to that. They feared a grievance or lawsuit would embarrass the school district, activate angry parents, and possibly cause a district to lose its federal funding, which could be a sizable 17 percent of a district's budget.

From watching Cookie, I learned diplomacy, charm, engaging rhetoric, and street smarts that I put into practice later in my Colorado House of Representatives political career. As a result of Cookie's leadership, thousands of Colorado girls have participated in high school sports and learned the joy, teamwork, time management, perseverance, and power that come from sport participation. This outstanding leader has won thirteen Hall of Fame recognitions too numerous to mention. Thank you, Cookie. The baton you handed to me will next be grasped by women I am mentoring for political office.

Cookie's partner, Kaye, officiated junior and senior high school basketball, and I encouraged her to learn officiating at the NCAA level, which she did. Kaye was the Naismith Women's Collegiate Basketball Official of the Year in 2014. James Naismith was the inventor of basketball in 1891 at Springfield College, MA, when athletes threw a ball into a peach basket attached to a high wall. Later the bottom of the basket was cut out, allowing the ball to fall through, and voilà, we had basketball. Kaye became a decorated NCAA official and evaluator of other officials and the ranks of women officials has increased dramatically.

Today, when I see professional women athletes like Serena Williams, Candace Parker, Mikaela Shiffrin, Megan Rapinoe, female sportscasters, referees, coaches, athletic directors, and college presidents, I'm humbled to realize that when millions of women and I spoke up saying that "something is wrong and we are going to fix it," our voices spurred massive social change. At the 1985 New Agenda conference sponsored by the Women's Sports Foundation and others in Washington, DC, I conducted a workshop titled, "Women Leaders for Women's Sports." This title caught fire with other women's sports leaders. Even though I had zero experience in coaching or physical education, I clearly saw the damage that the absence of female role models caused for young girls and the denial of athletic jobs for talented women all ready and eager to get a job with a strong career ahead for them. Thanks to the US Olympic Committee in Colorado Springs and the CDE, I was able to become a local and national expert on the letter and spirit of Title IX.

One highlight of my athletic leadership career was addressing two hundred women's collegiate basketball coaches in the Women's Basketball Coaches Association in 1983 at the storied Rupp Arena in Lexington, Kentucky. These women asked, "Will we really get paid a livable wage? Do our teams really get to use the weight room? You mean travel, uniforms, and shoes are paid for by the school, cheerleaders are actually required to perform at our games, and women sportscasters will be announcing women's games? You mean our players don't need to launder their own uniforms? You mean women will even referee in the black-and-white stripes?"

I looked into the eyes of future Hall of Famers like Tennessee's Pat Summit, Stanford's Tara Van Derveer, Texas's Jody Conradt, Rutgers's Vivian Stringer, Kansas's Marian Washington, Texas Tech's Marsha Sharp, and UCLA's Billie Moore, and shouted "YES!" High fives and cheers shook and rattled the historic arena all the way up to the second-level bleachers.

CHAPTER 11

Leadership Training for Girls and Women

At this 1983 women's sports New Agenda conference in Washington, D.C., I learned a valuable lesson. I was bitterly disappointed when only two professors attended my very important (so I thought) presentation. Why didn't three hundred women come to hear about "Women Leaders for Women's Sports"? Did this sound too radical and too feminist? But from this experience, I learned the power of speaking to a small audience, in this case, an audience of two. One woman was a college professor from Texas and a VIP officer in the National Association for Girls and Women in Sport (NAGWS). The other one, Dr. Christine Shelton, was a bilingual international sports professor from Smith College who served as a consultant to the Women's Sports Foundation. They both affirmed that "Women Leaders for Women's Sports" was an ongoing mission needing much more immediate and institutional priority.

Prof. Shelton taught at Smith College, the Ivy League institution I'd dreamed about attending when I was in high school. But on my telephone operator salary of 96 cents per hour, Smith was not in my future. But Prof. Shelton encouraged my work in Colorado with the CDE Women Leaders for Women's Sports project, and we took this battle cry to the NAGWS, to the national Women's Sports Foundation, and to the US Olympic Committee. Even though I was never a coach or physical education teacher, Chris had confidence in me. She could think outside the box and listened to what an academic feminist like me might have to offer.

As I looked around at girls' and women's competitive games, I wondered, where were the women coaches and officials? The women sportscasters? The women athletic directors? Such women were needed as role models in order for young girls and women to fulfill their career aspirations. Today, fifty years later, the catch phrase, "If she can see her, she can be her," is finally familiar. Women can be decisive, brave, intelligent, and powerful. Also, I learned that hundreds of women with excellent résumés were seeking head coaching jobs in their respective sports and hoped to establish careers in the sports they loved. Determined to support the goal of women leaders for women's sports, I wrote and published a gutsy manual titled *Sports Need You: A Working Model for the Equity Professional: How to Increase the Number of Women and Minorities in Athletic Coaching, Officiating, Administration, and Governance* (CDE, Schafer, 1984).

With encouragement from Prof. Shelton, legendary sport feminist Dr. Carole Oglesby from Temple University, and NAGWS President Dr. Mimi Murray from Springfield College I went on the speakers' circuit for this cause célèbre. This goal was beginning to catch fire in the nation's high schools, colleges, and at the United States Olympic Committee (USOC). Dr. Oglesby was a leader who listened to an academic feminist like me. Her book *Women and Sport: From Myth to Reality* (1978) was the landmark feminist textbook that inspired and validated my lofty goals for Colorado, the nation, and the world. To this day Dr. Oglesby continues to lead worldwide efforts for the safe and healthy participation for girls and women in sports from the US, to the United Kingdom, to Europe, Scandinavia, Asia, and Africa. Dr. Oglesby is a former co-chair of the International Working Group for Women in Sport (IWG). In May 2018, my partner, Barb, and I were privileged to attend the fourth IWG Conference in Gaborone, Botswana. Next up was IWG in Auckland, New Zealand, in 2022. These inspiring IWG conferences occur every four years with one scheduled in England in 2026.

With several coaches I had organized a Colorado network of coaches, officials, and athletic directors with the title of Educators for Athletic Equity (EAE). It became a model for other states seeking to publicize opportunities for women to train as coaches and officials, and to file grievances if the Title IX laws were broken. Equally important was the fact that the EAE included many highly respected male coaches and ADs, as well as fathers of girls who advocated for Title IX. Hundreds of fathers across the nation shouted at school board meetings, "What do you mean there's no volleyball or softball for our girls?" as they shook their fists at bewildered local school board members. Thousands of fathers became advocates for Title IX and full equality for their daughters and for other girls and women in sport.

The goal to have women leaders for women's sports has improved, but parity has hardly been reached. Because Title IX required strong salaries for girls' and women's sports, thousands of men have applied and have been hired, often claiming women were less qualified. Data from the WSF show that the percentage of women coaching women has declined since Title IX passed. Also, hiring authorities still practice subtle sex discrimination against women applying to coach female athletes. Some limited positive development is that in 2022, women comprised 66 percent of women's college basketball head coaches. How slow is progress.

While I was working at the CDE state office building I had noticed a thick gray rope dangling out of our fifth-floor window. Fifteen of us worked on the fifth floor and our director explained that the rope was the "fire escape" that we could use to slide down to the pavement if we were strong and not disabled. But we had two disabled colleagues who would never be able to slide to safety. Such was the condition of many state buildings, which were unsafe for hundreds of state employees.

After six months of advocating for a legitimate fire escape, one was installed, and I lost my chance to slide down the swinging rope. The aesthetics of the fifth floor consisted of orange shag carpets, ash trays in every cubicle, and empty inboxes until the crush of copiers and fax machines loaded them up. With no telephone answering machines back then, we took turns "watching the phones" for each other and writing down messages from callers on little pink slips. Now I wonder why we were "watching" the phones? I was curious one day when a strange purchase called a Radio Shack appeared on the fifth floor of the CDE. It was something called a computer, and twelve of us consultants and secretaries huddled around this miracle machine. Thankfully we learned how to use the basics of it, but all of us had to share the hours and sign up in advance to use it for our forty minutes per day. Of course, the secretaries were the fastest to learn the computer and tutored us consultants in its use.

I experienced many joys at CDE, and we were all excited and anticipating to celebrate the first Teacher in Space on January 28, 1986, at 9:39 a.m. MST. But from my experience as a private pilot, I became extremely alarmed hearing the morning television news that the temperature at Cape Canaveral, Florida, was barely 32 degrees, and it might be somewhat risky to launch the Challenger Space Shuttle. Even I, with only fifty hours of solo private flying knew the O rings on the shuttle could freeze when temperatures dropped below 32 degrees.

Whatever were those brilliant NASA scientists in Houston thinking? But mission control engineers asserted that freezing was not likely since the day temperature was going to rise to 50 degrees. But would the O rings thaw out in time for the shuttle's launch? I doubted it!

I yelled at the television, shaking my fists, and pounding on the TV to delay this fool's mission, please! My demand in Denver of course was not heard in Houston. Fifteen minutes later the shuttle blasted off, and after seventy-six seconds in the sky, the $3.2 billion Challenger Space Shuttle carrying six astronauts and a master teacher exploded. I heard colleagues gasping and crying because an outstanding teacher-astronaut, Christa McAuliffe, representing the hopes and dreams of millions of teachers and students across the country, perished in the explosion. Teachers who'd carefully prepared lesson plans about astronomy, the planet, and space were speechless trying to explain this disaster to young children. The expression from the mission control, "Houston, we have a problem," has sadly become a common slang for any problem in society, politics, and sports.

An ironic end to this tragic story is that my good friend and teacher Robert Stack from Greeley, Colorado, was bitterly disappointed when he was not selected as the Teacher in Space. He had been a finalist but thankfully has now lived another thirty years as a husband, father, science teacher, grandfather, and retired USAF colonel who has traveled the world with friends and family. I still mourn the loss of Christa McAuliffe and her fellow astronauts—what would they have accomplished and enjoyed in their lives?

Another painful day at CDE I'll never forget was the Columbine High School massacre of ten students and one teacher on April 20, 1999. Three colleagues and I were discussing standards-based education in the fourth-floor meeting room, diagramming on a white board how to help districts implement these new academic content standards. Suddenly a television blast from an adjacent room alerted us to deaths and horror that were unfolding at this wealthy suburban high school in Littleton, Colorado. Two male twelfth graders were exchanging gunfire with police while students and faculty hid under desks and in closets. The killers subsequently committed suicide in the school library. They were celebrating Adolph Hitler's birthday. I was so sad I could not finish the day and returned home to mourn.

Thus began this era of terrorizing young children, parents, teachers, and citizens with active shooter drills on how to protect themselves in the case of imminent attacks. And we as citizens and elected officials have found no way to stop the deadly mass shootings by mentally disturbed young men. The worst ones were at Sandy Hook Elementary School in Newtown, CT, killing twenty-six children and six educators on December 14, 2012. Another grisly one was in Uvalde, TX, at Robb Elementary School on May 24, 2022 when the shooter shot and killed nineteen children and two teachers. The shooters at both schools used AR-15 assault rifles, which can fire twenty shots in one minute. I'm just waiting for the next terror to happen, and still nothing is done about senseless gun violence. How many more innocent victims must die before our elected officials do something to stop this madness beginning with banning assault weapons?

Despite the tragedies I witnessed at CDE, I was thrilled with two projects my supervisor Jay and I initiated the Expanding Your Horizons conferences for middle school and high school girls, which exposed them to professional women in nontraditional jobs for women (e.g., doctor, engineer, plumber, police officer, minister, military officer, attorney, pilot, electrician, painter, etc.). Successful women in these occupations described in small groups how they trained for those jobs and encouraged the girls to think beyond the roles of teacher, nurse, or secretary. Although the speakers honored these important traditional jobs, they encouraged the girls to consider the hundreds of other occupations that might appeal to their interests and abilities. The girls learned that becoming a wife and mother was a desirable but unpaid position with no social security or health insurance benefits.

Similar to the Expanding Your Horizons conferences, Jay and I organized annual Women Preparing for Educational Leadership conferences. Numerous talented female teachers had never considered becoming a principal, superintendent, district administrator, or athletic director. Successful women already in those positions inspired and urged the teachers to "think and prepare big" to maximize their talents and improve the culture and experience for students. In the 1980s, approximately 98 percent of superintendents and high school principals were male, while 75 percent of elementary principals were male. Where were the highly qualified and talented women? Shouldn't these leadership positions be filled from 100 percent of the talent pool instead of just 50 percent of the talent pool?

Fortunately, in 2023 national data revealed that women are 38 percent of superintendents, 54 percent of high school principals, 39 percent of middle school principals, and 89 percent of elementary principals. Let school leadership reflect the composition of the student body—50 percent female, 50 percent male. Certainly, it is very important for little boys to see men as elementary principals and to see many more men as teachers. Men comprise only 11 percent of elementary teachers at a time when many boys have no father or positive adult male in their lives. According to the Centers for Disease Control and Prevention, boys are less likely to finish high school, are five times more likely to spend time in juvenile detention, and are more likely to be diagnosed with ADHD, attention deficit hyperactivity disorder. With 80 percent of the total teaching force being women, boys have very limited exposure to healthy, adult men and mentors. This is wrong and needs to be fixed. I wish every healthy American man could become a Big Brother to a fatherless boy, which would set that boy's life on a positive track.

I was asked by the commissioner of education to manage a large initiative—the development of new statewide academic content standards because a damning national report titled "A Nation at Risk" in 1983 documented that not all of America's children were making adequate yearly progress: children of color, children living in poverty, children with limited English proficiency, children with disabilities, indigenous and immigrant children. As I reviewed the civil rights social reforms from the 1960s to the 1980s, I was chagrined to learn such reforms had hardly resulted in equality and equity in education, which is a philosophical statement meaning all students have equal opportunity to learn.

Equity in education means, "What do the data actually show?" For example, the data show that girls but not boys read proficiently in grade three. There is no equity (according to the data) when boys are reading far below grade level, even though they have an equal right to reading instruction. Although reforms from the '60s to '80s paved the way for more stable lives for white middle class students, entrenched racism, poverty, hunger, drugs, and segregated schools frayed the safety net for children at risk. This was all wrong and I with others needed to fix it.

So the next major national education reform effort to fix these unconscionable problems was called standards-based education starting in 1990. To address these inequities through the new standards, educators were required to define exactly what must be taught, what must be learned, and what must students be able to do in each grade level and in each discipline. Assessments of student learning in reading, writing, and math showed that the at-risk groups were not actually making adequate yearly progress. Standards-based education focused on setting high expectations for all students and ensuring highly qualified teachers for all disadvantaged groups.

Blessed to have worked with many Blacks and Hispanics in the civil rights office at CDE and as the CDE director of the School Effectiveness Unit, I worried whether I had the ability and courage to undertake such a statewide responsibility. But first I needed to work with Colorado legislators to pass a bill requiring adoption of these academic standards with Colorado law HB93-1313 to include standards in reading, writing, and mathematics.

Before these statewide standards were adopted, schools and teachers would teach whatever content they thought was useful including the contents from dusty old files, outdated materials, and lesson plans often not tied to any agreed-upon topics. Schools were so underfunded it was no wonder that teachers didn't have updated materials. One jaw-dropping example was the use of 1960s globes and geography books that included countries that no longer existed. For example, some maps showed Northern Rhodesia as the country in Africa, which has since become Zambia. The old globes did not reflect how climate change had shifted rivers, oceans, mountain ranges, and human populations. Out-of-date textbooks forced hardworking teachers to select bits and pieces of information that may or may not have been applicable for students preparing for the twenty-first century. Until the standards were adopted, there was no uniformity across the state with regard to what should be taught and learned in every discipline and in every grade. For me this was another example of something that I and others needed to fix.

In addition to my professional life, I was also grateful for the growth of my daughters Mary and Annie in their academics, swimming, soccer, cheerleading, and positive friendships. Mary was a tall, thin brunette with sparkling green eyes, and Annie was taller and slender with brown eyes. They were happy with their father's new wife, who lovingly helped raise them, and with my partner, who was a gentle disciplinarian. One thing missing in the girls' lives, however, was Sunday school, something I regret to this day. Even though they were not exposed enough to sacred hymns and biblical texts beyond the Ten Commandments and the Beatitudes, the girls grew up to be moral and ethical young ladies, thanks to an extended family of positive adults and by the grace of God.

Both my personal life and my professional life presented many surprises and challenges. Thankfully my daughters with their gay activist mother were making strong progress in their personal and academic lives. Both girls graduated from the University of Colorado at Boulder and aimed at careers in finance. Mary earned an MBA at Columbia University, and I expect Annie will also soon earn an MBA.

what students should be taught, what should be learned, and what students should be able to do at every grade in the three R's: reading, writing, and arithmetic. But in English, "I will always teach the proven method of phonics and phonemic awareness," cried many English teachers—phonics meaning learning a letter or a pair of letters that makes up words and sentences. But other English teachers fought for the "whole language" approach, which today is largely debunked whereby pupils learn the whole word instead of by syllables.

Unfortunately today in 2024, educators still debate the best method for teaching reading while thousands of American children are not learning to read, jeopardizing their lives and futures. A recent report published by the *Washington Post* Editorial Board (March 11, 2023) regarding the "reading wars" said, "Cut the politics! Based on the research phonics is the best way to teach reading." Meanwhile sadly in the US in 2023 only about 40 percent of third graders are proficient in reading. Children who can't read proficiently by the end of third grade are not likely to graduate high school. This is a frightening forecast for our country's future. Conflicts also erupted among writing and mathematics teachers about what was important to teach, learn, and for students to be able to do in their disciplines.

Then even more fury was unleashed on Colorado lawmakers and me when teachers of science, history, geography, civics, economics, art, music, foreign languages, theater, dance, and physical education realized that their subjects had been totally excluded from the new law. "Just teach the three R's," less-informed legislators and school board members said. "We don't have the time and money to write standards for all those other subjects."

These opinions are all wrong and I will fix them, I said to myself. I led the efforts with the legislature and the state board of education to amend the bill to finally include those excluded disciplines. "Don't we need well-rounded students and citizens? Don't we need the arts, for example, that bring joy and beauty into students' lives?" I asked.

At one senate hearing, I testified on behalf of dance, which many officials had ridiculed. "Who needs dance?" they snarled.

"For every human ever born, rolling and turning in the womb is the fetus's first and most primitive movement experience," I stated. "A pregnant woman feels her baby rolling around and vigorously punching her abdomen with its arms and legs. Throughout human history, homo sapiens have been dancing, singing, drawing, and acting long before they were reading and writing." As recently as January 28, 2024 David Brooks wrote in the NY Times that music, art, literature and culture can save "a sad, lonely, angry and mean society." As important as the three R's are, there must be standards for all subjects that prepare students for a full, rich education and life.

Just to clarify: The thirteen content areas in Colorado are reading, writing, math, science, history, civics, geography, economics, music, visual art, theater, foreign language, and physical education. This combination of disciplines makes for a well-student and citizen.

Upset at the limited, antiquated thinking of many educators, parents, and elected officials, I also advocated for a modest interdisciplinary curriculum as taught in Europe, Japan, and Scandinavia in these high-achieving countries. But I encountered fierce resistance to this approach: "We can't water down our discipline by also teaching music and geography," proclaimed some of the three R's teachers. Or "I'm a math teacher and I don't have time to teach any economics!" Challenging these attitudes made me very unpopular with all of the three R's educators.

Naïvely I asked: "Doesn't economics require math skills? Wouldn't math be more engaging and fun to learn if it included hearing and analyzing symphonies, and even rap? Can you teach both? In social studies, would reading important stories from American and world history inspire students to appreciate the human journeys and prevent repeating errors of the past? Wouldn't examining a Picasso masterpiece motivate students to write about what the artist might have meant to convey?" Had the teachers been given assistance and training on how to teach in a modest interdisciplinary way, they might have been open to trying this approach. But in Colorado and other states, teachers are overworked, underpaid, have no aides, and are not given paid professional growth time to learn new strategies.

I soon became the anti-Christ to the leaders of the three R's hierarchy who considered themselves the guardians of their disciplines. The dam broke when I requested them to add persons of color to their standards and instruction discussions. They petitioned the commissioner of education to fire me. Even though this was denied, I had painfully learned how entrenched elitism and racism are in our society, even to this day. I recalled how my UNC graduate school professor in 1970 had warned us: "Any of you who challenge the guardians of the disciplines will be crucified." And I thought he was joking.

Unfortunately, this rancor over standards continued to divide my state content specialists who were actually master teachers. But these three R's content specialists wanted to fight to the death and not compromise or water down their most important three R's by teaching in a modest interdisciplinary method. After cooling down a bit, they asked, "Which disciplines should we prioritize, which ones should we minimize, and which ones should we erase?" This was a no-win situation for most of the disciplines; it was either/or thinking—apparently the three R's specialists felt they couldn't teach in a modest interdisciplinary manner. I was not advocating for a 100 percent interdisciplinary approach but for some reasonable small efforts.

Other consultants in my unit supported the interdisciplinary approach of including some of their disciplines in an interdisciplinary approach while also writing standards in their specialties—science, foreign languages, civics, history, geography, economics, physical education, art, music, theater, and dance. The battles raged on. The English consultant feared that some reading and writing would be taught by "ignorant" history and civics teachers; the math consultant failed to see that teaching at least some economics skills with math would help students save money and earn a living. The theater specialist, however, understood the value of the interdisciplinary approach and explained that productions like *Les Misérables, Hamilton,* and *West Side Story* were perfect opportunities to learn some history. Books like *War and Peace, To Kill a Mockingbird, Beloved,* and *The Silent Spring* like most all books have elements of many disciplines.

But the antagonisms led by the three R's consultants boiled over to the point that the commissioner eliminated my entire CDE School Effectiveness Unit, which he and I judged to be totally ineffective. As the director I felt and still feel like a total failure unable to find compromises to please everyone. But the loss of the unit was minor compared to the loss experienced by 150 small and rural schools in the state, which were left abandoned by the master teachers from my unit with no state leadership on best practices for teaching the thirteen disciplines.

At the last meeting of our ineffective unit, the commissioner announced, "Consultants, you're all released. Goodbye." Later he told me, "No one could manage such a toxic situation. You did your best and I have a new job for you." Thus I rebounded from this implosion by being appointed a regional accreditation coordinator, a position that proved to be one of the most rewarding of all my jobs. And at CDE I also had made lifelong friends like Jan, Janice, Siri, Evie, Ai, and Gerry.

Sadly, from the Nation at Risk in 1983, to Standards-Based Education in 1993, and to No Child Left Behind in 2014, education experts in 2022 found that American students were making mediocre progress. Because of the Covid-19 pandemic in 2020 with closed schools, remote learning, and disruptions of classes, educators worry that future declines are imminent and that the United States is still a nation at risk with millions of children left behind.

CHAPTER 13

Seeking the Gay Goddess

With all the responsibilities in my professional life, I felt it was past time for me to find joy—and to find the mythical gay goddess partner. My first gay partner and I separated in 1995. I started seeking a beautiful, intelligent, fit, and funny gay woman who also understood those creatures known as "teenagers." But where was she? Without electronic dating sites in the 1990s, how would I ever find this perfect SWF, single white female? Hang out in Denver lesbian bars like the Three Sisters or Ms. C's and spot a hot babe through the sweat and the smoke? Run a personal ad in the *Big Mama Rag* or *Outfront*: "Lonely lesbian mother of two teenagers seeking help to raise them." That didn't sound too inviting. Join a softball league of burly tomboy types or a women's chorus with singers who looked like hippies? Wander through the Gay Pride Festival wearing rainbow-colored socks and a purple T-shirt emblazoned with the slogan "I'm One Too!"?

The women's sports network, Educators for Athletic Equity, that I'd founded in 1984 came to my rescue. One of the female referees informed me that a certain Barbara Nash, who was an assistant principal at Denver West High School, was someone I should meet.

Hey! Hadn't I met her in an in-service class I taught—that cute woman in the bright green dress with sparkly blue eyes? Attired in high heels, with gold bracelets and perfect silvery fingernails, she kept interrupting my lesson plan as she tried to get my attention in the class. And she did. A week later my phone rang in Loveland, and it was the Barbara Nash. But was I brave enough yet to have a dinner date with a "big city lesbian"? I was just a "country girl" from a hick town fifty miles north of Denver.

Trembling with fear on our first date, I ordered creamy clam chowder and a Coors Light at McCormick's Fish House in Denver Lo Do, a busy upscale area. Surely big city lesbians would have an alcoholic drink, which I did only to be cool, even though I hated beer. She ordered a Diet Pepsi, no alcohol. I was attracted to her because she had bright-blue eyes, straight white teeth, and pinkish manicured fingernails. Such priorities. Did all big city lesbians apply lacquered shiny nail polish? How femme. Feeling nervous, I hid my broken nails and jagged cuticles under the table. We discussed literature, arts, politics, and world travel. She didn't wear blue jeans and a flannel plaid shirt with a heavy key chain, back then a.k.a. the "lesbian uniform." On our second date she twirled me around like Madonna at Ms. C's lesbian dance hall to Brooks and Dunn's "Boot-Scoot Boogie," K. T. Oslin's "Come Next Monday," and Anne Murray's "Could I Have This Dance for the Rest of My Life?"

Wow, I believed this lady had potential. She was a striver and a bit of a masochist pursuing a PhD in education administration. She also held a demanding assistant principal position in the Denver public schools. Trying to impress me, she revealed, "Since you were born and raised in Maine, you'll be pleased to know that my ancestors, including John Carver, the first governor of Plymouth Colony, came over on the Mayflower in 1620." Right! I had heard that old line many times before—all of Maine's one million residents' ancestors "came over on the Mayflower." With names like Schwab, Goldstein, and DiTullio? I don't think so. Enough of Barb's effort at status enhancement. Then I learned that she is from an East Coast West Point family whose father, Lt. Col. James Nash, served in WWII in the Pacific while my father, Lt. Col. Edwin G. Pierce, served in Europe. Thus we had values in common, except my ancestors didn't come over on the Mayflower. Most came from Scotland and Ireland as poor immigrant farmers working the land in Pennsylvania and Nebraska.

Years later, still questioning Barb's tired old Mayflower boast, imagine my surprise when I met her eighty-year-old aunt Gertrude Carver (wow) in Hartford, Connecticut, who drove us to the state capitol to show us a tarnished iron plaque hanging on the front stone wall. There was an etching of JOHN CARVER, GOVERNOR, PLYMOUTH COLONY, 1643. That's settled.

Moving right along, thank God, Barb didn't drink alcohol. I could not tolerate another alcoholic in my life. Cute, sober, witty, sexy. Quite the package. But I was unschooled in how to become a powerful lesbian. Could Barb teach me?

For example, on a road trip returning from the La Forêt church retreat in the Black Forest of southern Colorado, we stopped at a 7/11 store and parked a little too closely to a huge black Chevy Silverado four-by-four truck inhabited by a burly redneck who yelled at us, "Back off, muff divers!" Not missing a beat, Barb yelled back, "Back off, pencil dick!" He burst out of the cab ready to strike her, but his buxom blonde girlfriend wrestled him back in, shouting, "Bubba, she didn't touch your door and you can't get arrested again!" They sped away with wheels squealing through clouds of dust and tumbleweeds. Hiding quietly in the back seat, I peeked out, whispering, "Are they gone? What's a muff diver? What's a pencil dick?"

How naïve could I be? My polite New England and Kappa upbringing hardly prepared me for the "skills" needed for big-time lesbian womanhood: Take no bull from anyone, talk back, fight back, and don't mess with us. I started to learn how to grow a lesbian backbone.

I was sad to depart from Barb for a while. I had read *Zorba the Greek* and planned a trip to Greece with my fellow French teacher, Toni, a first-generation straight Greek woman. She'd asked me to accompany her to this country of ancient gods and wisdom on the Aegean Sea. "We'll visit with my aunt and uncle in a small rural village near Sparta where little English is spoken. As a history and geography buff, I was fascinated with how rural Greek people lived. And although there was no power or electricity in rural Sparta, Aunt Helena baked the best pita and moussaka in a wood-burning stove. How did she bake baklava in a wood-burning stove? And Uncle Boris served us retsina wine made from his small hillside orchard.

Always being a history and geography buff and eager to learn more about Greece, the cradle of civilization, years later, Barb and I took an all-lesbian Olivia cruise to Athens and the Greek Islands. My gay goddess Barb and I first walked along the boardwalk of the small Piraeus seaport with blue and white Greek flags flying from vessels entering and departing. Of course, we had to stop for tzatziki snacks and a glass of ouzo at a sidewalk café. Upon sailing to and arriving in Athens, we hiked up the steep hill to one of the Seven Wonders of the Ancient World, the Acropolis. I learned about the 2,500-year-old Parthenon citadel at the top with its Doric columns. Some geniuses of the ancient day realized that the columns needed to be narrower and thinner at the top in order to stand strong for the ages and to look parallel from the ground.

We next boarded the ship to the islands and realized that a lesbian cruise line with two hundred sporty lesbians was the trip of a lifetime, especially when we learned we would be visiting the original island of Lesbos. The welcome party on board featured flaming redhead hottie Wynona Judd as she belted out "Why Not Me?" and "No One Else on Earth." All aboard for Mykonos, Crete, Rhodes, Santorini, and Lesbos.

The hilly Greek island of Mykonos has one of the best views as far as the eye can see of the azure-blue Aegean Sea. I can imagine ancient mariners navigating through the storms, mist, and snow to reach its safe harbor. To enhance property values and ensure massive curb appeal, the Mykonos government chose pastel colors residents should paint their homes, so the hillsides were splashed with pink, lavender, peach, mint, and mauve to create visual beauty and peace.

As we anticipated finally arriving at Lesbos, the home of ancient lesbians and lore, the local government was afraid that real-life lesbians would be bad for business and scare away heterosexual shoppers. So the government banned our ship and hundreds of us tourists—missing out on a local shopping boom for one day. I learned that Lesbos has since changed its policies and now welcomes any and all visitors because, you guessed it, it's good for business.

Because Barb and I enjoyed history so much, we decided a year later that since Turkey also is a pinnacle of ancient history we should definitely visit this centuries-old country. While sailing into Istanbul in the golden dawn with sun shimmering over fifty domed mosques, we heard the mournful chanting of the Muslim call to worship echoing from ivory-colored minarets. Welcome to the country that straddles eastern Europe and western Asia, which explains the hundred languages and nationalities evident there. We first visited the storied Blue Mosque, the jewel of Istanbul that requires skirts and head scarves for women to enter. Luckily we came prepared. Women prayed in the back on the stone-cold floor, while men prayed in the front on cotton mats. White lights and candles hung and flickered from the massive ceiling, creating a solemn cavernous atmosphere. Millions of shimmering blue mosaics adorned the walls, creating a shiny, prayerful presence.

I wanted to tour the Grand Bazaar in Istanbul, the heart of the city, with its labyrinth of a hundred covered canvas tents and marketplaces. Arriving at the bazaar, I noticed Mercedes Benz and Rolls Royce cars parked in front while elderly, disabled, and blind locals sat on the sidewalk with their hats and baskets pleading for a donation or food. Tourists spent millions of dollars, euros, yen, and lira inside the bazaar but bypassed the beggars altogether. I was greatly bothered by this selfish behavior, and I dropped what I could into their baskets. I wished it could have been more.

I hate shopping of any kind, but Barb loves to window shop (as she calls it). Lo and behold, inside the bazaar she spied a ten-by-eight-foot purple, red, and black Persian rug hanging on a wall. Soon a tall, dark, handsome salesman appeared and, of course, guaranteed that the rug was a "wonderful bargain for such a beautiful and lovely lady." After sixty minutes of flirting and flattery, Omar made a great sale. And the treasure from the bazaar still warms Barb's office today.

As a history buff and tired of shopping, I was ready for the bus ride to Ephesus, another one of the Seven Wonders of the Ancient World. This ancient Mediterranean port city has well-preserved temples, libraries, and an outdoor amphitheater that has excellent natural acoustics and can hold 25,000 concertgoers. Christians and other pilgrims remember Ephesus from St. Paul's letter to the Ephesians in 30 A.D., in which he explained that the Christian gospel of love and salvation is available to Jews, Gentiles, and heretics alike. "Walk in love as children of God," invited Paul. Ironically, in 200 A.D., the

Romans started using the Ephesus amphitheater for bloody gladiator combats, and a gladiator graveyard was even unearthed there in 2007. So much for Pauls' edict to walk in love.

Lt. Col. Edwin G. Pierce and Pauline Hosack Haskell Pierce in Portland, Maine. Col. Pierce served in the U.S. Ninth Air force in WWII

Young Sisters Susan, Mary Elizabeth and Mother Polly Pierce in Portland, Maine.

Susan Pierce at Lincoln High School, Lincoln, Nebraska.

Sisters Mary Tate-Phillips and Susan P. Schafer, Ed.D. in Eugene, Oregon.

Kappa Kappa Gamma Sisters in Lincoln, Nebraska. Left to Right: Susie Pierce Schafer, Judy Erickson Gaylor, Ginny Wheaton Hallager, Sheri Jacobson Roos, Judy Luhe Farmer, and Patty Knapp Tweed.

Gary L. Phillips, Ph.D. in Portland, Maine.

Tennis players at Vail, Colorado. Left to Right: Audrey Meiggs, Ilsa Mahrer, Ava Meiggs, Barb Nash and Sue Schafer.

Susan's Partner Barbara L. Nash, Ph.D. and her brother James O. Nash in Denver, Colorado.

Son-in-Law Michael T. Meiggs, Daughter Ann Schafer Meiggs, Grand-daughters Ava and Audrey Meiggs in Keller, Texas.

Daughters Mary Schafer Mahrer and Ann Schafer Meiggs in Wheat Ridge, Colorado.

Barb and Sue on an Olivia cruise in the Mediterranean.

Colorado State Representative Sue Schafer and U.S. Senator Hillary Rodham Clinton in Denver, Colorado

Mary S. Mahrer, Ilsa O. Mahrer, and Nathan A. Mahrer on a beach.

Grand-daughter student Ava G. Meiggs in Keller, Texas.

Grand-daughter student Audrey L. Meiggs in Keller, Texas.

Grand-daughter student Ilsa O. Mahrer in New York, New York

CHAPTER 14

Modern Family Lives

Upon returning to Colorado, I wondered how this apparent gay goddess and potential life partner would tolerate zany, frilly teenagers. Having managed our early romance and experienced great joy and laughter, I wondered if Barb could pass the ultimate test—meeting daughters Mary and Annie, who worshipped Barbie dolls, fashion, jewelry, makeup, hair styles, cosmetics, disco, Neil Diamond, cats, ice skating, and cheerleading. With a little help from her brother, Jimmy Nash, Barb passed with flying colors. Jimmy was the dramatic, dashing Denver "hairstylist to the stars," whose philosophy was "The higher the hair, the closer to God" and "Beauty knows no pain." Having little interest in such matters myself, I was blessed that my teenagers met Jimmy, an expert on all things beauty and fashion.

I noticed how they devoured Jimmy's and Barb's advice on manicures, hair styles, eye liner, dating, and boyfriends. Barb helped the girls with homework and figuring out how to run a 10K race. Highlights of our excursions to Denver included trips to Jimmy's luxury salon at the Oxford Hotel, to the Ice Capades, and to Chuck E. Cheese. Introducing the girls to a bit of gay theater, we laughed at gender-bending productions like *La Cage aux Folles*, *Tootsie*, and *Mrs. Doubtfire*. Soon the girls said they were ultra "cool" being part of the gay subculture, even bragging that they could always tell a lesbian from a non-lesbian—yes, these savvy girls thought that they had "gaydar."

Our life as an extended family of two women and two daughters advanced on parallel tracks. The girls were ready for college, and Barb and I had reached the peaks of education administration—Barb as a middle school principal and I as a CDE director. Mary graduated from CU-Boulder with a degree in MCDB (molecular, cellular, developmental biology) and Annie graduated high school, then later delaying her CU graduation to spend a gap year in a Chicago art school while her CU boyfriend worked on a doctoral degree in anthropology. He was not, however, as compatible as she had anticipated as he was more liberal than her conservative views.

Mary fell in love with a gorgeous young man who Barb and I thought was gay. Mary's "gaydar" failed to extend to the male universe because this young man *was* gay, and Mary was disappointed but eager to meet some heterosexual men. She then accepted a number of high-powered finance jobs in San Francisco and New York City where she eventually met a straight and powerful single white male named Nathan. Coincidentally, Nate hailed from Pittsburgh not far from where my mother was born and raised. Nate even had Colorado roots, having graduated from the Colorado School of Mines before earning an MBA from George Washington University. Working in finance, Mary was convinced that an MBA from Columbia University would advance her career. So on a sunny spring day as tulips, daffodils, and lilacs bloomed around the university's cobblestone courtyard, Mary did earn her MBA.

I was worried about Annie's counter-culture boyfriend in Chicago, and she returned to CU to earn her BA in psychology and business. Annie volunteered at a women's safe house and interned at the CU counseling center. In Boulder she met an upstanding civil engineering student who was very much to her liking. Mike was a tall, handsome redhead from Colorado Springs. I was so happy (almost delirious) about Annie finding such a good man, I celebrated by racing out to the Acura dealer in Boulder and spent all my money on a new sporty A4 coupe.

Soon Annie and Mike became engaged and married on May 31, 2004, at the Boulder First Presbyterian Church. I was thrilled helping plan the wedding with Annie, a real mother/daughter effort that was so much fun I'll never forget it—what do we do about flowers, bridesmaid dresses, hair styles, music, hors d'oeuvres, drinks at the reception, and beef or salmon for dinner?

But before the wedding, however, some of my friends asked, "Do you think a lesbian mother and her partner can be walked down the aisle in front of two hundred guests and can even be seated in the traditional mother of the bride seat?" In the early 2000s homophobia was a factor to be considered—how "out" can gay people be, especially at a formal event like a wedding? Annie and Mike took a strong stand announcing that the lesbian mother and her partner would be walked down the aisle by Mike's brother, David, and proudly seated in the traditional seat for the mother of the bride—left side, front row, first seat in the row. I was thankful these two courageous young people would honor and respect the bride's mother and her partner. After the wedding Annie and Mike moved to Maryland, where Mike served as the chief engineer at Camp David appointed by President George Bush, and Annie worked in insurance and student loan offices.

Another highlight after the Annie-Mike wedding was daughter Mary's and fiancé Nate's wedding on a Colorado mountaintop at Keystone Ski Resort on August 20, 2006. These festivities started with a golden sunset hayrack ride and barbecue dinner hosted by Nate's parents, Joy and Doug. Of course, on the day of the wedding, strong winds, thunder, and rain started thirty minutes before Mary walked across the outdoor deck to meet her groom. What would we all do in pouring rain? Miraculously all bad weather halted just in time for the bride and groom to say their vows. (Yes, there is a God.) Unfortunately, some guests from sea level had become ill riding in swaying gondolas at 10,800 feet and missed the Dom Pérignon champagne, steak dinner, and disco dancing until 2:00 a.m.

With both daughters married and on their way to good jobs, Barb and I decided we would travel more. England's Wimbledon grand slam tennis tournament was the pilgrimage of a lifetime for devout lawn tennis worshippers. I wanted to pay homage to the greats of the game. Shaded by vine-covered walls and soaring white canvas tents, guests are served cocktails and hors d'oeuvres 24/7.

Starting in 1877, crowds have cheered at Wimbledon for such greats as Bill Tilden, Rene Lacoste, Suzanne Lenglen, and Helen Wills Moody. Strawberries and cream are still served with an almond crumpet and a pint of Guinness. Champions Martina Hingis and Jim Courier sat near us at breakfast and we even exchanged a few greetings. I heard thundering, clapping crowds on twenty green-velvet grass courts.

One day Barb asked, "Who are those seventeen-year-old African American sisters with pink and purple beads in their braids? Looks like they have promise." Right. "And that kid from Mallorca, Rafael Nadal, who we saw play at the Australian Grand Slam tournament in Melbourne is quite the talent." How prophetic. I had heard that the food in England is terrible, but we found fish and chips, Chinese stir fry, and chicken tikka masala to be mighty delicious. And the favorite beer in England is not Guinness, but none other than Bud Light.

Having had such fun in England a year later, we later flew to France and got very lucky. "Quelle chance!" as the French say. During the month of June 2009 at the Paris de Gaulle International Airport, we saw tulips and lavender blooming in planters while rainbow flags and bright-purple balloons fluttered overhead. Along the route to our hotel, thousands of rainbow flags streamed from cafés, office buildings, and the grand department stores. Apparently Paris was a very welcoming city for gay people. But nearing our Hôtel d'Arsenal close to the Place de la Bastille, the cabbie grunted, "No more taxi," and dropped us off with our luggage six blocks away because the International Gay Pride Parade had started. Walking several blocks toward the hotel, we heard the thumping, booming disco sounds from Donna Summer's "Hot Stuff" and the Bee Gees's "Staying Alive." We began to see sweating, shirtless muscle men wearing nothing but tight silver Speedos (or less) bumping and gyrating on floats and fire engines. I decided the first public bacchanal had started right before my eyes. Fierce and fabulous drag queens attired in pink floral rhinestone body suits and size fifteen gold high heels waved signs stating, "Vive l'amour, darlings!" Not to be missed and riding on sleek black Harleys, French "dykes on bikes" roared through the 14th Arrondissement on their way to the Arc de Triomphe.

We hadn't planned to attend one of the largest gay pride parades in the world, but there we were, celebrating Gay Pride International 2009 with one million European, Scandinavian, African, and American LGBTQs storming the City of Light. On another lucky day in southern France years earlier, I heard rumbles, motors, and screams at 6:00 a.m. from my small auberge because the Tour de

France cyclists were racing though at 9:00 a.m., and I had a second-floor perfect view. Other tourists and locals had camped out overnight to catch the greatest athletes in the world. How do they ride 140 miles (280 kilometers) up mountains and hills in one day and do it all again the next day?

Later back in Paris, Barb and I climbed the wrought-iron lattice Eiffel Tower, which weighs over 8,000 tons and stands proudly over the city. It challenged us to climb the 500 steel steps to the summit. Sadly we failed to reach the champagne bar at the top due to heavy, slow traffic on the steps, and parts of the tower were under construction.

After Paris we took a coach to a moving, spiritual area for us—the windswept Normandy region of the Omaha and Utah Beaches where thousands of WWII allies, including my father, halted the German assaults into western Europe starting on D-day, June 6, 1944. How the Allies scaled those treacherous cliffs with German artillery firing at them I cannot understand. Even on the sunny day that we were there, the winds were ferocious, blowing sand, rocks, mist, and weeds into our eyes. With the ocean roaring below, I could not hear any dangers above like the bombers back then that killed the ones climbing up the walls. I was moved deeply as I viewed the thousands of shiny white Christian crosses and white marble Jewish Stars of David, which reflected the gratitude I have for the 135,000 American soldiers who died in the Normandy battles. My father's US Ninth Air Force landed there on June 9, 1944, and proceeded to bomb the Germans' cannons and installations, which made their advances useless.

Such a busy summer, but we couldn't miss the Roland Garros Grand Slam French tennis tournament in Paris. We sipped iced café au lait and nibbled on chocolate croissants as we watched Steffi Graf, Roger Federer, and the King of Clay, Rafael Nadal, battle it out on the dusty red clay courts.

CHAPTER 15
From Horror to Joy

Everything was going amazingly well for me when terror and horror struck for millions of Americans and our allies. On September 11, 2001, at 7:20 a.m. MDT, I boarded a commuter bus from Lakewood, Colorado, to downtown Denver. Breathing the cool mountain air and enjoying the clear blue skies and golden aspen leaves, I thought that life couldn't be better. I had a loving partner, a good job, excellent health, a future secure retirement, and our home mortgage was almost paid off. What could possibly go wrong? Then I overheard the bus driver mumble that some plane had just crashed into a New York City skyscraper. What did some stupid private pilot do now? I said to myself disgustedly. Didn't he watch his navigation instruments, or couldn't he see with his own two eyes a 110-floor skyscraper?

Having earned a small private pilot license myself, I felt ultra-knowledgeable about the mistakes that amateur pilots like me make. For example, once flying over the San Juan Islands near Seattle I got lost in the clouds and had trouble finding my way out; another time I landed the wrong way on a woody rural airstrip, and I barely missed causing a head-on collision. Unforgivable. But that particular pilot error on that day in the New York City traffic control zone was outrageous. I waited to find out at my office what the idiot had done.

At 8:05 a.m., as I walked into the State Office Building, I heard loud radio blasts ricocheting across the marble walls and saw that my coworkers had tears in their eyes, as did even the commissioner. They were all glued to smoky television images of the American Air Lines Flight #11 jetliner slamming into the World Trade Center Twin Tower soon followed by United Airlines Flight #175 crashing into the second Twin Tower. Unbelievably, a third jetliner, American Airlines Flight #77, smashed into the Pentagon in Arlington, Virginia. With wet eyes, sobs, and hugs, we were immobilized by our grief for the innocent crews, passengers, and officers who died. Then we estimated that thousands of employees in the towers and hundreds of firefighters, first responders, and police officers had also lost their lives. A fourth American jetliner had been hijacked by terrorists and was somewhere over Pennsylvania. But the heroic passengers on board were able to attack the terrorists, which caused the plane to crash in a rural field instead of in the White House. The exact figures of fatalities that day were 2,996 employees; 300 firefighters; 200 first responders and medics; 70 police officers; and 55 Pentagon personnel. A tragic day that lives in infamy.

We learned a terrorist organization named al-Qaeda led by Osama bin Laden of Saudi Arabia had financed and plotted the hijacking of these aircraft to kill thousands of Americans. This attack was the deadliest on American soil since the bombing of Pearl Harbor in 1941 that killed 2,400 US Navy sailors and precipitated the United States' entry into World War II. We wondered how the Pentagon, the bastion of supreme military world power, could be the victim of a surprise attack right next to Arlington National Cemetery where over 300,000 American war heroes are buried. Where was American intelligence?

From Horror to Joy

Then while grieving the massive destruction and the thousands of lives lost, I was shocked to suddenly realize that my NYC daughter, Mary, and her husband, Nate, often attended meetings in the two fallen towers! Were they among the casualties? How could I find out? Also, my daughter, Annie, was driving en route to Maryland where her husband, Mike, was stationed at Camp David. Could Camp David also have been a terrorist target? Were my beloved daughters and sons-in-law dead or alive?

Truly terrified, I called their cell phones: no answer, no power. I decided to call the girls' father to see if he had heard a message from Mary or Annie, who both might be in harm's way. But the medical secretary at his office failed to believe me—that there was an emergency, or that I, Sue Schafer, was the mother of the doctor's two daughters. Reluctantly, she interrupted him. He was with a patient, and when told about his daughters' risks, possible injury, or even death in a terrorist attack, said nonchalantly, "Well, let's just see about it." I understand many working people may not have heard the news of the terrorist attacks starting at 7:30 a.m. Mountain Daylight Time.

"Death to America" and "flying airplanes into American buildings" were just idle threats and "exaggerations," according to some overly confident military commanders, scholars, and politicians. Our leaders never imagined in their wildest nightmares that an American aircraft would be hijacked and used as a weapon of mass destruction. Dr. Madeleine Albright, the secretary of state, loudly and often contended that rogue states like the Islamic State and al-Qaeda must be taken precisely at their word with their "Death to America" threats. Dr. Albright had traveled extensively across the globe and had continually urged military leaders to take idle threats very seriously.

Frantically trying to call Nate, Mary, Annie, and Mike on their cell phones to learn if they were okay, I received no answers. None.

Beset with fear and trembling, I was, of course, unable to concentrate on any office work. After four long hours, Nate finally emailed me the best news of my life: "Mary is safe." Nate was safe. Mary later sent me an email saying, "Mom, don't worry about me; pray for the people who really need it. I love you, Mary." Annie was delayed in Annapolis, Maryland, where she was on her way to see Mike, the Chief Engineer at Camp David. But she had to spend three days with total strangers and then learned Mike had actually been deployed to Naval Base Guam. I was so thankful, so relieved, so overjoyed. Annie was later able to fly to Denver and then back to New York City to celebrate her birthday on September 27, 2001, with her sister, Mary. So my beloved daughters and sons-in-law were safe but scarred forever with horrible memories of 9-11-2001.

But what about the thousands of other parents, spouses, children, aunts, uncles, grandparents, and friends of victims who lost their family member or friends in that fiery collapse of iron and steel? September 11, 2001, has changed the course of history. No one should complain when they have to wait in the airport TSA lines or notice video cameras on major US and foreign streets. Security officials are working to prevent us from terrorist attacks and I am grateful for all they do.

As lovers of the sport of tennis but with fears of jetliners colliding into buildings, Barb and I got up the courage to fly to the Australian Grand Slam tennis tournament in Melbourne. My entire life I had wanted to attend the four Grand Slams of tennis—the French, Wimbledon, New York, and the Australian. So we were ready and boarded ourselves into a "sardine can" next to the toilets on a Qantas Airlines flight for sixteen long hours. Finally above Australia, we were delighted to see blue and white waves crashing on the golden beaches of this largest Pacific island. Australia is a large, flat, dry landmass of three million square miles originally inhabited for thousands of years by Indigenous people. I was angry to learn the British invaded the land and established the first white colony by sending prisoners and criminals there and brutally destroying most of the Indigenous cultures. With tickets to the Australian Tennis Open, we were ready to watch the best players in the world. Amelie Mauresmo from France is gay, and she won the championship. Gotta love that Justine Henin from Belgium with the best one-handed backhand in the world. How does she do that?

Several days later, I said, "Let's go snorkeling on the Great Barrier Reef!" Bad idea. We paddled and splashed but then, oops, we swam too far out and got trapped in the rip tide. In the rip tide you are paddling furiously and going nowhere. Lifeguards had to rescue us back to the snorkeling deck. Luckily the guards treated us and other losers to the best cookies in the world, Tim Tams. (Tim Tams have two layers of creamy light chocolate spread between crispy, flat dark chocolate cookies, now even available at your local grocery store.)

Since it's 95 degrees on a typical Australian January day, Barb and I wanted to experience a jungle picnic, called a "barbie" where the temperature would be cooler, like 90 degrees. The barbie offered tropical fruits like lychee and jackfruit. Lychee is round with sweet white, scented flesh and is even used in martinis! The ripe jackfruit is sweet and often used for desserts.

Barb suggested that we go to New Zealand since it's only a three-hour flight from Melbourne. So we hopped a flight to Auckland on the north island, which is tropical rather than the south island, which is more like our mountainous Colorado. While there we learned that native son and hero Sir Edmund Hillary was the first person to summit Mount Everest in 1957 and that the sheep industry is one of the largest in the world, with one sheep per person. I won notoriety and envy by being the fastest contestant in our tour group to catch a lamb and feed it a gallon of milk from a fifteen-inch plastic baby bottle complete with a nipple.

We admired the Indigenous Aboriginal First Nation villages and their muscular warrior dancers who commanded our admiration with drums and shouts of war cries and of battles won. I appreciated that a wool/possum mix sweater felt like cashmere and was one of the best buys for a bargain-hunting tourist. Who knew that possum fur was so soft and warm? The Kiwi cuisine is unique in the world. "Hangi" sounded terrible, but it is a native dish made from crayfish, lamb, and root vegetables cooked in a pot over an open pit that gives the meal a smoky, earthy flavor. When traveling I needed to be courageous and try new foods, and Hangi was no exception. Hangi tasted even better with a glass of Marlborough Sauvignon Blanc.

One year later wanting to travel somewhere where they also speak English, we flew to Dublin in Ireland. After arriving in Dublin, we traveled 150 miles by coach to the Cliffs of Moher where we were hit with a blast of blinding wind and pelting rain on the cliffs. "Where is this Emerald Isle?" I asked. All I could see was fog and sleet, and I was soaking wet. But a few hours later on our coach, we saw the Emerald Isle's carpets of green pastures stretching past two-hundred-year-old stone farmhouses. "But how in the world do people stay warm in those ancient stone homes?" I asked. The locals explained that the houses retain heat very well after giant foam insulation is sprayed in. As academics we were excited to visit the Dublin Writers' Museum featuring James Joyce, Oscar Wilde, and George Bernard Shaw. We even saw some of their original manuscripts! I bet these gentlemen would be pleased to add today to their ranks Frank McCourt and Maeve Binchy.

Later Barb the English teacher demanded that we visit Trinity College Library in Dublin. Founded in 1592, it has over 100 million books, manuscripts, films, journals, and maps—and the Brian Boru harp from the 1400s. How do you preserve a harp for 600 years? And this harp is the national symbol of Ireland. For someone who worships libraries, this one towers over all the ones I've ever seen. I admired the hundreds of aisles and floors crammed with historic artifacts. Next we motored to Waterford, Ireland, to see how the craftsmen fired glass that creates luxurious crystal goblets, bowls, decanters, and chandeliers. Artists wore industrial plastic shields over their heads and eyes and held fiery steel rods that rotated on a large piece of glass to shape a product of function and beauty. At the entrance of the factory we saw a five-foot-tall Waterford Lismore crystal claret glass that weighs one hundred pounds and sparkles in the overhead pink and lavender lighting. The owners of the factory have a sense of humor because there's a small sign near the base of the glass that says, "If you break it, you buy it for only 30,000 euros" (approximately $30,000). Of course, the world recognizes the most famous Waterford production—the six-ton crystal geodesic ball in New York's Times Square that drops at the stroke of midnight, ushering in the new year.

CHAPTER 16

From Education Careers to New Adventures

Many years earlier, Barb and I were known as a modern family, with the girls' father, his wife, Barb, and I advancing our careers while also enjoying the girls' schooling, friends, and activities. I remember cuddling my newborn daughters, mesmerized by their sweet faces and their kicking arms and legs and wondering what in the world would they become. A high school or college dropout? A teenage mother? A drug addict? A rebellious runaway? Cancel those thoughts! I was remembering Merry in Philip Roth's classic novel *American Pastoral*. In spite of the best middle class and parental upbringing, Merry chose to run away only to be found homeless, doing drugs, and living under a bridge with an unemployed alcoholic boyfriend. Could such an outcome happen to our modern family? Thankfully, by the grace of God, Mary and Annie were solid, healthy teenagers.

Barb reached her multiple goals of earning a PhD, becoming a middle school principal, running a marathon, climbing fourteeners (Colorado mountains over 14,000 feet), rescuing a dog, and traveling the world. Soon I started dreaming of tackling something larger than public education. I had tried to fix as much as I could for education reform, sports equality for girls and women, for civil rights in schools, and for uniform academic content standards. My goal of becoming an assistant commissioner of education, however, was brutally thwarted by the arrival of an arrogant, right-wing, sexist new commissioner. I had heard of bad bosses and bosses from hell, but fortunately, not until late in my career was I forced to report to a real live tyrant. We called his tenure the reign of terror.

The new commissioner didn't want any women in his weekly leaders' meeting. He didn't remember any employees' names except those of a few white men in the top echelon of the department. He wouldn't even say hello to another person in the elevator. No more holiday or birthday parties; no thank-you notes for a job well done. He abolished my unit's rebellious master teachers saying that "one hundred fifty underfunded small and rural school districts will just have to learn the instruction of standards by themselves."

In retrospect, this man was a pathetic harbinger of something far worse to come in 2016—Donald Trump, the malignant narcissist. My bad boss even looked like Trump, with bleached blond hair, baggy suits, long red ties trying to slenderize him, a fake Boston accent, and the alpha male swagger. For him it was way past time to bring back white male supremacy to Colorado education and society! Too much of these civil rights, women's rights, immigrant rights, Indigenous rights, disabled rights, gay rights, and that ultimate insult to white male supremacy, that African American president, Barack Hussein Obama. Enough already.

Sometimes, however, a shock delivered by a cruel, uncaring boss who downsizes jobs can have a silver lining. In my case, I changed from the school effectiveness director to an accreditation manager. My mother had always said, "Honey, when something bad happens to you, it's because God has a better plan for your life." And she was right. God was good to me by reassigning me to Dr. Roscoe Davidson, a kind, elderly, former superintendent-of-the-year who was named the new CDE deputy commissioner. I was able to retain my director rank and salary and continue to use my skills with superintendents across the state. The only things my new angel boss didn't like were computers. "Don't email me, just see or call me!" he requested. But he did not care for office birthday parties, which was all right with me. He considered these to be a waste of time.

Suddenly I started receiving phone messages from this new boss about what a good job I had done at the Western Slope curriculum directors' seminar, how well I had edited his press release, and how he appreciated my comments at the metro team meeting. Then he asked if I would coordinate the meetings of the Denver Area School Superintendents Council, a humorless, muscular group known for criticizing everything coming from the state legislature and from the CDE. Dr. Davidson recognized that I had the personality and temperament to deal with these leaders as they understandably struggled to lead severely underfunded and understaffed school districts.

Dr. Davidson demanded that all employees take their accumulated vacation days. One year, on my vacation days, Barb and I decided we would travel to Montreal for Thanksgiving. Barb stated, "That city isn't that far away. Vendors will be preparing for Christmas, so it'll be festive, merry, and bright, right?" True, but the November daytime high in Montreal is a frigid 20 degrees Fahrenheit. But when we arrived, we couldn't see any department stores, cafés, bookstores, or theaters, and decided that Montreal must be a large, boring city. Surely that couldn't be.

Finally we asked a friendly pedestrian where the action and the city center were. "Just go down those long escalators on the sidewalks.

You'll love it. There are restaurants, coffee shops, bookstores, luxury stores, singers, guitar players, concerts, sculptors, police, and military officers," the local man said. Montreal's population is 1,700,000 citizens, and it certainly did come alive with hundreds of them underground with us. And if you were hungry, there was French onion soup with croutons and grated Swiss cheese, tourtière meat pies, split pea soups topped with dumplings, cheese croissants, and baguettes packed high with ham and butter. Have a Syrah red wine or Molson beer with those. Because hotel personnel, shopkeepers, and waiters speak French, I was able to practice my Canadian French, which is spoken much more slowly than the frenzied French language spoken in Paris.

On our return from this trip, we had to spend a night in New York City before our flight to Denver the next morning. Then the most unexpected thing happened. Daughter Mary had said for many years that Nate and she *never* wanted a baby. So when my cell phone rang at 9:00 p.m. and Mary announced, "Hi, Mom, guess what, I'm pregnant!" I was shocked. I dropped the phone, rolled out of bed, and fell to the carpet thinking that I'd been dreaming. Barb picked up my phone and confirmed the good news: a baby daughter would arrive in early December 2013 on the NYC Upper East Side. I was one of two daughters, had two daughters, and decided it was time for a grandson. Apparently there were no Y chromosomes from my sons-in-law. And whether their offspring were X's or Y's, I was thankful all the grandchildren were healthy and fit.

A similar occasion had happened five years earlier when daughter Annie invited Barb and me for coffee at the Common Ground Coffee shop in Denver. I thought it was a bit strange for her to issue an "invitation," but after taking a few sips of my hazelnut latte I was told that she had something special to tell me. Speaking coyly, she murmured, "I am with child." Me? I was going to be a grandmother? I pictured myself with curly white hair, scaly thin skin, bifocal spectacles, and orthopedic shoes sitting in a rocking chair while feeding this miracle grandchild a bottle of warm milk. How did I, *me*, ever get this old? But I just knew that this infant would be the most beautiful, the most brilliant, the most talented, and the most athletic child ever born to mankind. And she was along her cousins all known now as my granddaughters.

One year later we decided to use our vacation days to venture to Ecuador, Peru, and the Galapagos Islands. Ecuador is known as the middle of the world, the center of the earth, with 50 percent of the land mass being above the equator and 50 percent being below. Hotels and cafés are filled with yellow and purple orchids, and the scent of pink roses wafts through moist, cool air. If you like chocolate (who doesn't), coffee beans, bananas, and roasted guinea pig, you'd love Ecuador. Quito, the capital, is constructed on an ancient Incan city and known for its sixteenth- and seventeenth-century churches and structures that blend Moorish and Indigenous features. Beautiful!

Best of all, Ecuador is the gateway to the Galapagos Islands, which are full of shiny sea lions whose pups can swim at birth but cannot see. Miraculously the pups who weigh only thirteen pounds when born can hear their own mother's unique squeals among hundreds of other moms on the beaches. How do these pups do this? I remember sitting on a sunny, sandy beach with two black, slippery two-hundred-pound sea lion mothers called cows by my side. Soon their older twenty-pound pups, hearing their mom's voice, circled me and wanted to play. I was advised to not get too close to a pup lest a mom attack me. Meanwhile, the male sea lion bulls were out at sea, splashing and fighting each other while competing for the ladies. But we never did learn how a pup could find its own mother just by the sound of her voice. Many mysteries in the animal world.

We spied the white-headed albatross screaming and diving headfirst off limestone cliffs to catch squid and krill. And blue-footed boobies? That can't really be blue. Wrong. Their six-inch-by-six-inch feet are deep blue, like the azure sky. Giant tortoises slowly crawled along the volcanic rocks while gray and white mockingbirds screeched at us from above. Our guide Gustavo warned us to look where we stepped. "Marine iguanas are camouflaged on the rocks and they bite." These ugly, scaly, three-foot-long green and brown prehistoric lizards scared even the bravest of travelers. Meanwhile back on the ship all the women (and one man) fell in love with Gustavo, a tall, handsome, muscular Peruvian who at a few dinners wore bright-white Navy uniforms with gold buttons and gold braids. He was stunning and sexy even to us gay women. Sigh.

Next we journeyed on to the Peru Cuzco region, which is home to the massive Amazon rainforest and the ancient Inca citadel of Machu Pichu, 8,000 feet above the Urubamba River. Machu Pichu is a UNESCO World Heritage Site consisting of over two hundred dry stone houses, temples, baths, and cemeteries constructed on grassy green terraces. But there's no need to mow the grass because herds of brown and white alpacas do the job. The Incas abandoned this site in the 1400s, and it was rediscovered in 1911 only when a professor from Yale spoke with an elderly farmer who told him, "There's just a pile of rubbish over there." But beginning with a small excavation, this curious, determined professor found remnants of one structure that led him to believe there might be more buried underground. He later brought expeditions including students to the area, and year by year, they unearthed more buildings until the entire vast citadel was uncovered. These buildings were hardly rubbish.

But we'd hardly had our fill of all things Spanish. "Since Colorado has so much Spanish influence," I said to Barb, "Let's go see the rest of Spain starting with Madrid with its parks, plazas, palaces, and the Prado Museum." Madrid is the capital and the economic and cultural center with a population of 3.3 million. Although the Prado was crowded and magnificent, we found the Museo Sorollo to be charming with Impressionistic art pieces. "But there's much more to Spain than Madrid. So let's journey on to other exciting destinations," said Barb. Near Granada is the formidable Moorish Alhambra Palace and Fortress constructed on a hill with fountains, mosaics, gardens, streams, temples, art museums, and sculptures. Such history and grandeur earned it a UNESCO World Heritage site designation, and you had to leave your passport at a booth at the entrance so no unauthorized or risky persons could steal it or enter the fortress.

Next stop was Seville, Spain, which is known for flamenco dancing, singing, and the best tapas on the continent. Also I'd read about something called a cathedral in a mosque, but I thought that must have been an error. How could a Christian cathedral be located in an Islamic mosque? We found out in Córdoba. One part of the mosque has a huge cathedral in it, and it even has a very small synagogue in one corner. We noticed how Christian crosses, Muslim crescents, and Jewish stars of David were all visible and transcendent. If only these major religions could respect and pray together instead of fighting and killing each other. I pray someday this will happen.

CHAPTER 17

More Aspirations

I was tiring a bit from travel, so it was time to return to CDE, but I also wanted to seek some different types of educational work. I found it in the Denver Public Schools as a consultant in the social studies professional development department. Such a challenge! How do teachers teach world and US history, civics, geography, and economics in a curriculum that prioritizes reading, writing, and mathematics for the state assessments? We in social studies decided we could no longer teach so many facts and instead needed to instruct big concepts in all the disciplines along with major important facts. In the age of computers, it is easy to find millions of facts, but students need to learn to think critically, like applying, analyzing, synthesizing, and evaluating knowledge, including major facts.

I later took a stimulating job as an adjunct professor at the University of Denver (DU) where I prepared master teachers for what they needed to know about academic content standards when they became principals. I became an expert on academic standards and was often asked questions about them by legislators, lobbyists, and journalists. Learning what legislators did had motivated me to consider giving politics a try. Why not me? Then I met my own state senators and representatives and imagined myself in those positions because while at CDE I had analyzed drafts of bills, written fiscal notes (what a proposed law would cost the state), and testified in senate and house committee hearings. Back home I had organized my local precinct for electing Democrats, but was that enough? Hardly.

Then one sunny spring day in 2006 at CDE, one of my best friends Janice and I walked across the avenue to sit on a marble bench in the rose garden of the Colorado State Capitol. As I gazed up, admiring the gray stone pillars and the shining gold dome, I informed Janice that I aspired to become a state representative in that historic building someday. Such audacity—such determination—such daring and dreaming. But was it possible? I was scared. Then Janice immediately jumped up and told me how she would help me achieve my goal. As a professional life coach, Janice guided me every step of the way. I decided then and there to start scaling up to eventually run for elected office. So many things are wrong in Colorado—let's fix them.

First I transitioned from the CDE to my new job in the inner-city Denver Public Schools (DPS) and then to the University of Denver. I embraced the opportunity to learn about the lives of 80,000 mostly low-income, ethnic minority DPS students speaking over one hundred world languages who attended these schools. I was refreshed by this diversity, but I also realized that the resources hardly matched the needs for these students. And in comparing the public schools to the private University of Denver (DU), I noticed the DU buildings had thick carpets, giant overhead screens connected to the professors' computers, marble walls, self-flushing toilets, internet access, and microphones at every desk, as well as Whole Foods and Starbucks Coffee in the student cafeteria. What a contrast to many of the public schools where I'd seen cracked concrete floors, dripping pipes, scratchy blackboards, canned cafeteria food, out-of-date textbooks, and boilers that would sometimes blow up.

Not yet running for elected office yet and after retiring from DU and the DPS, I decided to take two years to travel the world because running for state representative would be a massive, full-time, unpaid job. I wanted first to see a variety of countries and cultures, and fortunately Barb and I as intrepid adventurers agreed. We started with Panama and Costa Rica. We were first warned that Panama City is a drug-infested area with high rates of thefts and murder. But Panama City was actually a sunny, tropical metropolis with lush flower gardens, palm trees, and sparkling waterways. We drove through Panama on our way to Costa Rica, but first we were excited to experience one of the Seven Wonders of the Modern World, the Panama Canal. Wow! The canal, which connects the Atlantic Ocean to the Pacific, saves commercial ships from having to sail 8,000 miles around Cape Horn to deliver their cargo. We boarded a ship with four high decks to travel through the canal for forty-eight miles in eight hours and learn how the locks work by opening or closing gates that change the water levels. While standing on the upper deck and looking down I expected to see a lot of waves and turbulence and to hear the banging of the fourteen-foot steel blades and teeth. But no, the locks all operate quietly and seamlessly.

We saw an 80,000-metric-ton oil tanker coming up behind us and prayed that the very low level of water would actually rise high enough to lift it. Miraculously, the tanker rose easily and quietly with seemingly no effort. And we didn't even see or hear much water splashing or sloshing around. Now we understood why the canal is one of the Seven Wonders of the Modern World. I wondered if a giant nuclear-powered aircraft carrier like the *USS Nimitz* could pass through the canal, and the answer is no. A carrier is usually 134 feet wide while the maximum width of the Panama Canal is 110 feet.

Having been charmed by the Spanish cultures in Ecuador, Peru, and Panama, we wanted to visit Costa Rica also. At the first breakfast in our San José hotel's cantina, I sat down drinking coffee and spotted a woman across the room who looked just like a friend from fifty years ago at Lincoln High School in Nebraska. I walked nervously to her table and said: "Hello, are you Jackie from Lincoln High School?" Jackie stood up and said, "Yes, what a coincidence after fifty years!" We agreed that it is certainly a small world. We enjoyed strolling on sandy beaches with palm trees shading us from the blazing sun.

Later, while hiking in the jungle one day, we heard chattering parrots and screaming howler monkeys. One of the howlers was furious with us for disturbing her peace and quiet and urinated on us; we thought it was just raining.

"Who wants to hold a cute little bat?" asked Lola, the field ranger at the bat museum in San José. She reassured us by saying, "Just hold your hand out for this sweet little blood-sucking rodent. It won't hurt you because bats only eat mosquitos and flies." This was not very comforting—and what was I doing at a bat museum when I could have been drinking a margarita at a local cantina? "Just don't get one near your hair," she then advised. (I was thinking of an Alfred Hitchcock horror film here.) Wanting to demonstrate how fearless we females are, I shouted to myself, "I am woman!" and held out my hand. A fuzzy, frightened, little gray vampyriscus with two wide, jagged, eight-inch wings rested on my shaking hand for a full eighty seconds. Yea! I love bats, but enough is enough. Curiously, not one of the macho men volunteered to hold an innocent little bat. What's wrong with men? I remembered in Cambodia not one man in our group wanted to have a cute, fuzzy tarantula crawl up his arm. Maybe these men think such things are silly?

Two years later in early 2010 before Mary and Nate's daughter was born, my telephone rang, and Mary and Nate asked Barb and me, "How would you like to fly to the Holy Land in November with us?"

"Yes, of course!" I exclaimed. Barb politely declined.

I have a passion for studying religion and even on an occupational interest test in college, I tested highest for becoming a minister. So my life-long dream had always been to visit the Holy Land and to learn more about Judaism, Islam and Christianity. This was one of my most-cherished trips. When I arrived at the JFK Airport for check-in to Tel Aviv, I heard mentions of "first class" and assumed it must be for the blond maven dripping with jewels and furs in front of me. But no, my generous daughter Mary and son-in-law Nate had purchased first-class tickets for the twelve-hour flight for me and also for Nate's parents. I certainly enjoyed sleeping in private "tents" for the long flight to Tel Aviv, but sleeping soundly was difficult because flight attendants kept plying us with offers of Godiva chocolate, Dom Pérignon, and spicy shakshuka, the Israeli specialty of a nest of eggs, tomatoes, green peppers, onions, garlic, and paprika served with a warm pita. Such was my first and only first-class flight. But no complaints.

Upon landing in Tel Aviv, our first stop was at the International Center of the Baha'i Faith located in Haifa on a high cliff. Nineteen garden terraces sprouted purple lilacs, orange lilies, and bright-red geraniums. Lemon trees blew gently toward the Mediterranean Sea while golden domes and bright-white arches guarded the sacred site. Curiously, Baha'i believers are safe from the Israel-Palestine conflicts, apparently because they believe all people are equal under one God, and because the generous Baha'is operate large charities in both Israel and Palestine.

While in Tel Aviv, one of the most gay cities in the world, had my family and I had known about the "gay rainbow walking tour," we would certainly have stopped at several bars to sample Carignan Blanc from the Judean Hills or the Yarden Katzrin merlot from the Golan Heights. All Israeli wines are kosher, and they delight people throughout the world. The highlights in Israel for me were the Old City of Jerusalem with the combined locations of the Muslim Dome of the Rock, the Jewish Western Wall, and the Christian Church of the Holy Sepulchre nearby. We witnessed a baptism at the church, hundreds of Jewish worshippers and tourists at the Western Wall, and devout Muslims praying over their beads at the Golden Dome. I inserted a tiny paper prayer at the wall that read, "I pray for peace and love for all God's children everywhere."

Suddenly, above the Western Wall plaza, a large Brazilian gospel group appeared with drums and blaring trumpets. Carrying Christian crosses and dressed in their nation's colors of green, yellow, white, and blue, they started marching, clapping, and singing, "Hallelujah!" Even the Muslims and Jews stopped and cheered them on, everyone shouting hallelujah. This parade was followed shortly by an even larger bar mitzvah crowd of Jews wearing their blue, black, and white shawls. They were honoring a thirteen-year-old boy who, according to tradition, had become a man that day. Witnessing the joy and respect shown by these three major religious groups to each other, I could only pray that this respect and love would spread throughout the world. No more hate. No more violence. No more persecution. Let's just celebrate the same God we all three worship with our central belief of love.

Next, Mary and I stood on the banks of the legendary River Jordan where John the Baptist baptized Jesus of Nazareth and the Israelites crossed into the Promised Land. Although I am not a charismatic

Christian, I am awed by the stories of what this river has meant throughout the ages. It flows 156 miles south from the Sea of Galilee in northern Syria to the Dead Sea, which is actually a salt lake below sea level.

We were blessed when we saw a congregation of sixty Baptists from Oklahoma wearing white robes being individually and gently submerged in the river by their minister. Other Baptists on the banks were singing, "Praise God from Whom All Blessings Flow" and "Let's All Gather at the River," while taking photographs of their fellow wet and baptized believers. What a picture for Facebook, right? Apparently you can rent robes on the riverbank for a donation of 45 shekels or $5.00. Mary and I considered this opportunity, but we heard that the River Jordan is muddy and cold. Yet even if it chills the body, just being there did warm our souls.

Later we stood in the breezy, grassy field where Jesus delivered the Beatitudes at the Sermon on the Mount and emphasized that God's children should practice mercy, compassion, generosity, humility, and love. We were certainly on sacred ground.

CHAPTER 18

It's Not a Job. It's a Calling

Returning from my two-year gap from paid employment and international travel, I seriously reconsidered my teenage life's mission of "Something's Wrong—Let's Fix It." Seeing how hard elected officials work just to get elected and then to work fifteen-hour days, some weekends, and even holidays, I realized that such a goal could not be a job but a powerful calling. I was passionate about things that needed big-time fixing: insufficient funding to fix low-income and rural schools; inadequate medical and mental healthcare; crumbling roads and bridges; discrimination against Blacks, Hispanics, Indigenous people, women, disabled, and gays; gun violence; homelessness; pollution and contamination of our land, air, and water. Could I help fix these?

I remembered sitting on the capitol bench with Janice and looking up at the shiny gold dome. Yes, I shall do this. But I had no idea what it would take. It turned out to take all my time, courage, determination, energy, health, intelligence, and to neglect my family and friends. But something kept calling me to take on this challenge. I can do much but only with other committed citizens God willing. Of course this goal was a steep climb, much harder than climbing the fifty-eight fourteeners in Colorado. Having climbed ten of these including the highest one, Mount Elbert at 14,440 feet, I convinced myself that I would be able to push and persevere to win an election and pass laws for the good of all Coloradans.

Where did I ever get the audacity to even consider serving as an elected official? Was it my grandmother, Mary Daugherty Hosack, who served as a committee woman in the 1930s for the Republican Party in rural Pennsylvania? Was it the early encouragement that came my way when I was thirty-five years old in 1984 when a Colorado State Representative Steve Erickson (R-Loveland) knocked on my Lake Drive door to say he was running for re-election to the Colorado House of Representatives? We discussed the needs for K–12 and college education, and we brain-stormed ideas for healthcare, highways, business, and agriculture. At the end of our one-hour talk, Rep. Erickson suggested I run for an elected office. "Are you kidding? I have two children, I commute to Denver to work, I'd never have the time to raise money, walk door-to-door, telephone fifty people a day, or write detailed position papers for the *Loveland Reporter Herald* or *Denver Post*!"

But somehow, this crazy encouragement from a stranger, and a Republican no less, lodged in my subconscious for decades. Steve saw something beneficial in me and planted a seed in my mind I might never have considered. This seed lay dormant for thirty years until I reached the retirement age of sixty-two with many enticing paths ahead. Lesson learned: Our words have power to affect and shape other people, to do good or to do bad, even through many decades. Thus I take every opportunity for talented people to shoot for the stars, be bold, consider all options, follow your star, and follow your passions. You only live once; do it now.

But if I were to serve in an elected position, shouldn't I know the elected officials right here where I reside in Jefferson County, Colorado? Although I aspired to become a state representative, I had no clue what one does in that role or how they even get elected. Then one day while considering my possibilities, I received a postcard with the Colorado blue, red, and yellow flag printed on it from a Democratic lawyer running for the Colorado Senate in 1995. "Come meet Ed Perlmutter at a Broncos football party on Sunday afternoon," it read. This is what state representatives and senators do?

After shopping extensively for just the perfect fashionable ensemble to meet a candidate running for the senate, I was attired in my finest red and black plaid blazer, black slacks, silky red blouse, panty hose, shiny red leather pumps, and carrying my very official leather briefcase. With my heart nervously pounding, I arrived at Valente's Pizza Pub in Wheat Ridge, only to find a raucous crowd of 150 Democrats ranging in age from fifteen to ninety, wearing orange Denver Broncos T-shirts and blue jeans, and drinking Colorado's finest Rocky Mountain Coors beer. "Where is this Mr. Perlmutter," I asked an elderly woman in a wheelchair.

"He's over there," she said, "in the John Elway T-shirt leading the Broncos cheers."

Was that how a future state senator should be acting? Was that the proper attire for a state senator? Then at halftime, this Ed Perlmutter stood up on a shaky wood chair and gave a fiery speech about what Colorado needs to do to improve its health, its economy, its agriculture, its transportation, and its public education. With deafening chants of "We want Ed," crowds of admirers accidentally knocked him off the chair, thankfully caught him, and hugged him. I waited my turn in line to meet this Ed, and when I introduced myself and told Ed my address, he cried, "Great, you live in Paramount Heights? We need volunteers up there!" Volunteer? Paramount Heights? I didn't even know the name of my neighborhood or what a volunteer would do. If I were to become a serious political candidate, I certainly had to learn such important details and hundreds more.

On my way out the door, I asked a bearded supporter wearing bib overalls and a John Deere bill cap how a person gets involved in the Democratic Party. Chewing on his last corn chip, he mumbled, "Just contact your PCP." Okay, great, but whatever is a PCP?

I soon learned that a PCP is a precinct committee person for one small precinct. What does a PCP do? And who is my PCP, or my state representative, or my senator for heaven's sake? I soon found out.

Suddenly I was recruited as the PCP when I showed up at a small meeting and no one else would take the volunteer job. I did some rapid on-the-job training with other county PCPs. Our job was to get out the vote (GOTV) in our neighborhood, raise money for candidates and walk door-to-door advocating for them, recruit volunteers to phone bank for them, host house parties so neighbors could meet them, and most importantly make sure a Democrat is elected in every competitive race. This is a lot of unpaid work! Do I have the time? I decided to do these duties in my PCP role and must have succeeded because next I was elected as a precinct captain responsible for five precincts. After success in the captain role, I was unanimously elected as the House District 24 chair responsible for GOTV in ninety precincts. Even though all these jobs were non-paid positions and very time-consuming, we did them for our lives, our values, and for our future.

Soon enough the House District 24 Democratic volunteer "trainers from hell" cornered me. "You'll be leading the GOTV efforts and raising money for our Democrats to win every race up and down the ballot," dictated bulldog Polly Pinkston and taskmaster Roger

It's Not a Job. It's a Calling

Egerdahl. Polly and Roger were union activists and would fight until the end to stop a Republican from ever winning in House District 24.

Then these trainers from hell informed me a year later that since I had been a PCP, a captain, and the House District 24 chair, I should seriously consider running for a future state representative position. I was terrified of such responsibilities! But first, to get some experience, they planned meetings, appearances, speeches, and ten-hour workdays for me to make calls, organize fundraisers, walk door-to-door to get out the vote for Ed P erlmutter and to re-elect State Representative Moe Keller. Success! Both Ed and Moe won by large margins. Our House District 24 and I were even honored as "GOTV champions" in Jefferson County. When Ed termed out as a state senator and was elected to the US Congress, Moe was elected state senator followed later by my friend and mentor, Sen. Cheri Jahn.

Although afraid of running for office, losing, and disgracing my party, I did run for my first public office in 2008 and soon learned that a successful campaign required a "PhD"—managing paranoia, hypertension, and sometimes depression. My Republican opponents were out to stop me. Campaigning also forced me to learn more about human relations, having a positive vision for the future, fundraising, technology, politics, civics, economics, and laws. Before the age of computers and smart phones, we used hard copy "walking lists" and "phone trees" to meet, call, and identify likely voters along with organizing Friday Afternoon Clubs (FACs) to meet the candidate. Coffees at Starbucks and local potlucks did raise some money, but the FACs proved that "the more they drink the more they donate." A campaign in 2008 required raising $75,000; today in 2023 that amount would be over $125,000.

But here was a very serious obstacle in my first 2008 campaign—another determined Democrat challenging me in a primary. This meant I would have to work twice as hard—first to win a primary and then to defeat a Republican. "How dare a man who attended Democratic fundraisers mostly to eat tacos and drink beer challenge me," I muttered. Although this Democrat was a judge with a law degree from an Ivy League university, he proved that it is possible to have a high academic IQ but no common sense and zero EQ (emotional intelligence).

For example, reports came back to me that he had told voters that they should vote for him because he was a lawyer and that Sue was "just a teacher." Whoa. He had also stated that there were already "too many women in the State House." Really? Such ignorance was repeated even to women and other voters who ranked teachers as the most trusted of all professionals. Where did lawyers rank? Lower than door-to-door salesmen. My hardworking opponent had undermined himself so badly that, even working very long hours, he self-destructed and I managed to win the primary by a mere twenty-nine votes. You often hear "Every vote counts," and I proved it. I earned the nickname "Landslide Sue," which later catapulted me into the 2008 general election.

How do you win an election walking and campaigning in a snowstorm or in the blazing sun trying to meet potential voters? Of course many of these voters have a dog in their yard, but is it a friendly or dangerous dog? What I laugh at now was my encounter with a salivating sixty-pound pit bull racing out from behind a large, fenced yard. My only experience with a dog back then was with a twelve-pound Boston terrier puppy named Patsy Cline that I had recently rescued and had completed a dog obedience class. (Patsy earned an A; I earned a C.) And I'd mastered only two commands: "Sit!" "Stay!"

So when this barking pit bull charged at me, I froze, pointed my shaking finger at him, and bellowed, "Sit! Stay!" Shocked, the animal

It's Not a Job. It's a Calling

reared up on his hind legs, twisted his head in confusion, sat down, and panted for air. I dared not move one inch. Soon the dog's muscled, bearded owner, wearing a black DEAD T-shirt and standing on his front porch, shouted, "How did you do that? I've been trying to train Brutus to sit and stay for nine months." I slowly backed up, and still trembling I stated to him quietly, "Pet Smart classes, sir."

Thanks to Miss Patsy Cline, I'd learned how to manage both friendly and menacing dogs. Also I mailed a colorful photo of Patsy and me on paper fliers, which turned out to be a huge asset for me; many citizens informed me that they voted for me because "Patsy is so adorable." Whatever works.

Another frightening campaign experience occurred one day when I knocked on a voter's door and asked for "Carol," a Democrat living with her Republican husband, "Jack." Carol wasn't home, but Jack, a six-foot-two, stocky repairman with a can of Schlitz in his hand, opened the door and invited me in to talk "some serious politics." I was nervous with an odor of marijuana in the house and Jack's 200-pound drinking buddy, Bubba, sprawled out on a couch watching NASCAR on TV. Both men sneered at this lone female Democrat campaigning for office but lured me into the foyer by insisting that Carol "would be right back." I couldn't just back out, that would be rude.

Number one skill to defuse a potentially hazardous situation? Listen, reflect back the statements, say, "That's a point worth considering," and ask questions. They lectured me for over thirty minutes saying, "Democrats are communists full of corrupt union bosses, illegal immigrants, uppity feminists, faggots, and welfare queens." Frightened and thinking my life might be in danger, I desperately looked outside a window and around the room cluttered with ash trays. Suddenly I noticed a dusty antique Rod Laver tennis racket hanging over the fireplace with a few six-inch plastic tennis trophies placed on the mantel. With eyes wide open, I naïvely asked, "Where'd you get that classic wooden tennis racket, Jack?"

Jack: What do you mean, where did I get it? From Wimbledon, 1970. How would you know about tennis?

Sue: Oh, you guys play tennis?

Jack: I do. Not Bubba.

Sue: Where?

Jack: Oh, at a club in Lakewood, Colorado. You wouldn't know Meadow Creek.

Sue: Sir, I play tennis at Meadow Creek in Lakewood.

Jack: You do?

Sue: Sir, yes, I do play tennis at Meadow Creek.

Jack: Are you a rated player?

Sue: Yes, sir, a 3.5.

Jack: You're kidding! Have a seat! Would you like a beer?

Sue: No, thank you.

Jack: How about an iced tea? Coke?

Sue: Coke would be good. Have you gentlemen been to a tennis grand slam tournament?

Jack: Me, Wimbledon. Bubba here, none.

Sue: I loved Wimbledon and Roland Garros in France too.

Jack: Wow, you've been to two?

Sue: Four actually. Wimbledon, the Australian in Melbourne, the French Roland Garros in Paris, and the US Open in New York City.

Jack: Say, lady, we're needing a woman sometimes for our mixed doubles league. Are you ever available?

Sue: Yes, just give me a call.

Jack: Great! By the way, you are okay for a Democrat.

Sue: Sir, I am a pro-business, moderate Democrat.

Jack: Well, lady, I'll be voting for you. I don't know about Bubba.

Carol never returned and Jack never called me for mixed doubles.

Another risky situation for a gay candidate in the 2008 era arose one sweltering humid evening at 7:00 p.m. when I knocked on the door of eighty-seven-year-old Mrs. Smith. (My walking list gave everyone's age.) I calculated that since she was that old, I'd discuss topics of concern for elders: grandchildren's K–12 and college education, transportation options for seniors, stopping elder abuse, and protecting Medicare and Social Security.

I never wanted anyone to inquire about my personal life because being a gay candidate in 2008 was fraught with risks, forcing one to be secretive about one's personal life. Being a known homosexual could deep-six my campaign. I often could hide my gay orientation by using "heterosexual privilege"—photographs of my two children which I carried everywhere. With such documentation, no one would suspect I was gay, right?

When Mrs. Smith opened her door, I smelled ginger and hoped she might possibly offer me a ginger cookie. She was wearing a house dress and bifocals and asked me to sit on her front porch swing and offered me iced tea and a cookie. So far so good. But she showed no interest in any of the senior topics I had so shrewdly practiced nor did she want to see a picture of my two daughters. On her front porch with a gentle breeze breaking the heat, she and I engaged in this conversation.

Mrs. S: Honey, sit down in this rocking chair. I just have one question.

Sue: Yes, ma'am?

Mrs. S: Are you married?

Sue: Er, no, ma'am . . . I'm divorced. And I have two children.

Mrs. S: Well, do you have a partner?

Sue (getting nervous here): Uh . . . well . . . yes, I do have a partner.

Mrs. S: **Male or female?**

Sue (sweating): Er . . . well, er, ma'am, er, well, she's a woman.

Mrs. S: **GOOD! That's what I should have done sixty years ago!**

On my final canvass in the dusk of election eve, I, of course, wondered whether I would win or lose. I'd weathered eighteen months of campaigning in snowstorms, with frostbite, sore feet, sunburned skin, rattlesnakes, dehydration, vicious dogs, and neglecting my family and friends. But then, there it was—a bright, shiny rainbow stretching in the pink twilight from the foothills of Golden to the cornfields of eastern Aurora. Surely it was an omen.

CHAPTER 19

Novice Legislator and World Traveler

The election results were slowly coming in on a giant television on November 4, 2008, at 7:30 p.m. We Jefferson County, Colorado, Democrats gathered at the Holiday Inn in Golden. I saw everyone drinking champagne among sweaty hugs and sloppy kisses. I heard cheers amid red, white, and blue balloons floating over the ballroom. There was cheap wine-in-a-box and Coors beer flowing into plastic glasses, and chips and salsa were devoured by all. Did this mean I had won my election? Actually Barack Hussein Obama, an Illinois US Senator and author of *The Audacity of Hope* had just won the presidency! The first African American elected president was such an articulate, intelligent, talented, and gracious gentleman. Then, oh yes, someone named Sue Schafer had won as the Colorado State Representative from House District 24 for Wheat Ridge, Arvada, and Edgewater.

Although overjoyed at having won my first election, I was suddenly struck with, what do I do now? A philosopher once said that the greatest joy is in the journey, not the destination. I would soon see if that was true. I was mobbed by volunteers, donors, and supporters asking me what laws I'd get passed. By 2:00 a.m., I was dizzy and blinded by fatigue, and my feet were burning in my five-inch heels. But I was able to navigate my way home, mostly sober but delirious. The next morning, after a sleepless night, I woke up and pondered, whatever do I do now?

Problem solved. At 7:45 a.m. the next morning and after four hours of sleep, I picked up my cell phone: two lobbyists and one constituent were lining up to get appointments with me. George, the lobbyist for the Colorado Cattlemen's Association, thought that since the Wheat Ridge High School's mascot is the Farmers, my highest priority would be agriculture, and we needed laws to protect the beef producers. The next caller was a new constituent, Mr. Benson, requesting that I fix a law that had allowed his daughter's murderer to get off easy. Could I change this killer's time in prison from fifteen years to forty years? A Ms. Vigil representing audiologists requested to have coffee with me ASAP! Then at 8:01 a.m. the State House Services Office called to inform me that the new member orientation would begin Monday, November 17, 2008, from 8 a.m. to 5 p.m. in basement room 107 of the Capitol. No parking available. BYO lunch.

"Hey, can't I even have two weeks off to recover from the twelve months of canvassing neighborhoods in snow and tumbleweeds, getting lost in cul-de-sacs, contracting skin cancer on my nose, being chased by vicious dogs, dialing for dollars, speaking at fundraisers, and writing policy answers to the twenty questions that the *Denver Post* printed and distributed to one million voters?" I grumbled. The work had started before I even drank my first morning coffee. This didn't look like the glamorous job I envisioned, but I was determined to excel in this job as a State Representative.

During my first legislative session in 2009, I was expected to do "other duties as assigned" by the Speaker. I was assigned one wonderful duty to escort an energetic group of four legislators from Germany who were visiting our state capitol and the Denver Art Museum. I drove them to the Botanic Gardens and then out to see the Golden foothills. They requested a real Colorado meal, so I treated them to lunch at the Buckhorn Exchange. But no one ordered elk, yak, or Rocky Mountain Oysters. They did rank Coors Beer almost as good as their Pilsner. And they insisted on reciprocating my hospitality when Barb my partner and I could visit Berlin. Two years later, Barb and I did visit Berlin. The German legislators Eva and Karen took us to the underground Holocaust Museum, which is a stone labyrinth of interlocking blocks. Once in it, there was no visible way to escape, and for over ninety minutes we were frightened—we felt like we were trapped in a Nazi concentration camp. As a history buff, I needed to see Checkpoint Charlie, which marked the place where East Germans broke through the Berlin Wall in 1989. What joy for the East Germans who finally united legally with their parents, brothers, and sisters in West Germany. The legislators guided us on a tour of the stately Bundestag Parliament and later treated us to lunch for the Berlin specialty, which is curry wurst, a fried pork sausage sandwich, seasoned with spicy ketchup and curry and of course sipped with white Gessinger Zeltinger wine.

    These German legislators next escorted us to the annual Rite of Spring, the Berlin Outdoor Festival. Hundreds of elected officials, VIPs, and citizens came to celebrate the beginning of summer. Walking among vats of potato salad, rows of hanging sausages, and dozens of baskets of rye bread, we heard live polka bands and yodelers singing, "Ein Prosit." But the festivities came to an abrupt halt when a man in lederhosen shouted, "There she is—the Chancellor is here!" Barb and I pushed our way through the crowd to get a glimpse of short, stocky Chancellor Angela Merkel speaking to the adoring crowd. I was thrilled as a legislator and history buff to hear what Dr. Merkel would say. What an honor! What a strong role model she was for me! But why were these Germans all laughing? I didn't know that Dr. Merkel could crack jokes; she always looked so serious, even frumpy, on the political stage. Since Barb and I didn't speak German, we didn't get the jokes, but the Berliners were cheering and laughing, nodding their heads while lifting their beer steins. This short, muscular woman with red hair charmed Germans and Europeans everywhere with her no-nonsense, intelligent and strategic sense of direction for the entire continent. I later read Merkel's biography and learned that in order to pay for her college education, she had been a bartender for four years while majoring in physics and later becoming a Ph.D. physicist. Three cheers for bartenders.

I had run on an agenda of fixing things that were wrong, and I will briefly explain how a person can change, improve, and/or fix things. Fixing things requires three general skills, which I will over-simplify for the sake of brevity: 1) personality, 2) vision, and 3) knowledge. First, *personality* means being friendly, likable, outgoing, and smiling. The classic self-help book *How To Win Friends and Influence People* by Dale Carnegie is as good today as it was way back in 1937. Second is the skill of vision. Vision means seeing a positive outcome of a problem and explaining why it needs to be fixed, who can fix it, how will it be fixed, when will it need to be fixed, and estimating how much it will it cost in finances and volunteer and employee hours. The third skill is knowledge about the problem. For example, if a person wants to organize positive outcomes for homeless people, one would need to research why the problem needs to be solved and when, what is already being done and what more could be done, what causes this problem, what has worked and what has not worked, what it will cost, who will work on solutions, what homeless people say they need for physical and mental health, jobs, addiction treatment, and family and pet services. Reading articles and gathering research of complex problems will enable a person to propose positive outcomes for homeless people and for the area in which they live.

During another year in the legislature, I needed to practice the three skills of personality, vision, and knowledge as described above. I was never perfect in any of them, but I did my best to be a lifelong learner. But needing a break from "problem solving" when I had no re-election campaign, my partner Barb and I decided to travel internationally. Off we went first to Norway, and later south to Botswana and Mexico City. The descriptions below are oversimplifications of these rich and diverse countries.

As a history and geography buff I wanted to journey to Norway on the North Atlantic. But why? It has dry, salty, tasteless food and a strange language no one can understand. But wait, yes, Norway has steep ice fjords and emerald-green mountains that plunge into the ocean. But first we had to motor past Finland, the Arctic Circle, and to an actual reindeer farm where the Indigenous Sami ranchers raise hundreds of bucks, does, and fawns that graze in pens. But some reindeer run wild, don't they? Not any longer. Mostly they are all raised like cattle and provide healthy protein for millions of Scandinavians. Still some of our tourist friends could not even think of eating a reindeer steak or stew. But they changed their minds when it was 20 degrees outside, dark at 5:00 p.m., and we'd been traveling all day on a jolting bus in pouring rain. Hunger took over, and the travelers admitted that a hot reindeer stew is delicious, especially when sipped with Akvavit or Brut Arctic Cloudberry Wine.

Sailing down Norway's west coast, I saw fishing villages, oil rigs, and cobblestone streets with wooden houses. White-tailed eagles flew overhead trying to steal some cod or mackerel that were drying on racks. How do these people farm on such rocky shores? Cabbage, carrots, potatoes, and squash seem to thrive there. But the locals' favorite meal is a mutton/cabbage stew flavored with peppercorns; me, I preferred fresh, pink salmon with lemon juice while sipping that cloudberry wine. Much to the dismay of Barb and other travelers who didn't care for fish, every meal and snack started with fish—breakfast, midmorning snacks, lunch, happy hour, and dinner served with more fish, fish, and more fish. Luckily on this ship, there was a pizza café where the anti-fish contingent could at least have pizza or hamburgers.

I learned that Norwegians and Swedes are very competitive in politics, military, and sports. They like to laugh and make fun of each other. Our Swedish guide, Matt, told this joke about the Norwegians: It seems that a young couple in Oslo, Norway, had just bought a new house and were very happy until one day they went to their garage and found a group of raccoons living in there. They were distraught and called the wildlife officer, who advised them to just boil up a bucket of lutefisk and leave the pot in the garage for a few days and that will certainly drive the raccoons out. (Lutefisk is a whitefish left in lye for two days that is smelly, nasty-tasting, and has a gelatinous texture that most Norwegians dislike.) Two days later, the officer contacted the couple and asked if the raccoons were gone. The young man said, "Good news, bad news. The good news is that the raccoons are gone, but now there's a family of Norwegians living in there." Another joke was that Norwegians eat so much fish that they're growing gills. And according to Matt, the Norwegian national motto is "In Cod We Trust."

As a geography buff, I stayed up until 1:30 a.m. to catch the northern lights: flashes of bright lime-green and yellow swaths of clouds across a sapphire-blue sky. On another night, I saw the midnight sun with vast streaks of gold on pink, purple, and crimson clouds. Cruising south along the rocky Norwegian coast on the mighty Hurtigruten working ship, we crossed the Arctic Circle at 66 degrees north latitude. The good news was that you can be initiated into the somewhat "prestigious" Order of the Arctic Circle; the bad news is that the next morning after crossing the Circle you must stand out on the frigid, windblown deck at 10:00 a.m. and swallow a tablespoon of cod liver oil just as the ancient mariners did to keep themselves regular. No way! But desperate to join this fairly elite society, and having been promised champagne upon completion, I took a deep breath and gulped it down as fast as I could. Success. I earned a stainless-steel tablespoon shaped like a sturgeon for this miraculous accomplishment.

Oslo, the capital of Norway, is a unique city built in a forest that is entirely public land; even private property owners live on public land. Go figure. It's also the site of daring ski slopes; imagine flying off a snow-packed ramp that's higher than the Eiffel Tower. It's understandable why the world record for the longest ski jump distance is held by Stefan Kraft, a native son. Norwegians are very proud of their Viking heritage as seafaring warriors and as skilled traders, weavers, and craftsmen. Oslo's museums are filled with restored giant Viking ships, antique harpoons, and taxidermic whales. (Not sure how they brought heavy whale bones into a gigantic shed.)

I am still a history and geography buff, and in another non-election year for me, we traveled to the southern hemisphere and were invited to travel to Botswana. "Botswana? Where is that? Get a map. It's in Africa? Might be dangerous. Why would anyone go there? Can't afford it," we declared. But thankfully, we threw caution to the wind and attended an international women's sports conference in the capital, Gaborone, with my mentors, Dr. Christine Shelton, sport feminist icon Dr. Carole Oglesby, and Dr. Darlene Kluka.

One thousand African, Asian, European, Scandinavian, Canadian, and American women from eighty countries came together to fight for girls' and women's sports safety and equality. Two hundred workshops were offered, world champion athletes spoke, and marimba/drum and gospel concerts entertained us every night. Earlier when we arrived at the Johannesburg airport, I noticed we were the only white people in a crowded sea of Black Africans, and it felt very strange to stand out. What did I expect? I was in Africa, you idiot. Now I know how many Black Americans must feel in our country where they are often the only people of color in a group.

Soon we prepared for a safari to the Moremi Game Reserve and to the Okavango Delta, which is a UNESCO World Heritage Site. There we saw herds of grazing elephants and zebras wading and cooling off in a river, chubby warthogs chasing antelope, and a smash-faced mother water buffalo trying to hide her calf who kept peeking out behind her. Skinny, endangered wild dogs showed off their patchwork coats of bright orange spots and their huge brown ears. Stately giraffes towered over all. One hundred species of birds, like the rare lilac-breasted warbler with eight colors on its coat are found mainly in Botswana as well as the largest African elephant population in the world. The pitch-black Botswana sky was colored with bright glowing gold, blood-red, pink, and purple clouds.

At dinner I dined on maize porridge, a Seswaa meat stew with onions and peppers, Kalahari mushrooms, and Kgalagadi beer. Upon returning to our vine-covered motel where donkeys grazed outside our window, I was exhausted and frantically searched for my medicines and prescription drugs. They were nowhere to be found. I chastised myself: Just where did I put them? Did I leave them on our Botswana Airlines flight from Johannesburg to Gaborone? I'll never get them back, and I won't be able to sleep for the next ten days. Maybe I can borrow some Xanax from Barb in order to get a little sleep? Not likely. Why call the airline for such a lost cause? But call them I did, and a cheery Tswana voice answered: "Are you Susan Schafer? Sure, we have the bag with them right here, madame." God bless Botswana Airlines; they did the impossible even with thousands of international tourists getting on and off their airplanes.

Two years later, I was advised by many friends, "Don't go to Mexico City—there's so much smog and crime there." Hey, Barb and I live in Denver where there's smog and crime, so fortunately we disregarded this advice. On our first night in Mexico City, we ventured out on a tequila pub crawl (sounds dangerous), which ended at a large cobblestone public square. Hundreds of lovers, families, teenagers, and tourists listened and danced to six mariachi bands spread around a plaza festooned with green, white, and red Mexican flags fluttering in the breeze. It was a warm, starry night, and we were alive with joy. At one bar, while enjoying beautiful Mexican women singing and those dark, handsome mariachi musicians wearing tight black pants, silver belts, and silver metal botonaduras, I unfortunately consumed a bit too much tequila. I lost track of my tour group, which had left without me to go to one of the plaza's twelve cantinas to dine on mole, chicken enchiladas, and margaritas. Our eighteen-year-old tour director, my fellow tourists, and even my life partner, Barb, had all deserted me in this exotic, buzzing city.

I worried if I might be associated with the "businesswomen of the night" who were smoking cigarettes on street corners and dressed in bikini pants, black fish net hose, and strapless bras. For forty minutes, I waited on the corner for my tour director, friends, and Barb to retrace their steps and rescue me, but they did not. So I walked along the main avenue and eventually spied a police station. Yes. Was I saved?

At that point, our young tour director named Javier finally noticed I was missing. Panicked, he called my cell phone and told me not to move an inch because he'd lose his job if he ever lost anyone on his tour. After ten minutes, he found me and forcefully held my arm, leading me back to the Cantina Matador so he wouldn't lose his job. There I received stink eyes from the group, and even from Barb. I know I can't hold tequila and I should have been more careful. The only sympathy I received was from a fellow tourist who told me she got lost on an Easter Sunday in Rome at St. Peter's Square with 10,000 worshippers. It took her almost a day to find her husband. Looks like things could have been worse. Since then, however, Barb has decided to put me on a leash when I'm drinking alcohol out in public.

After this first memorable night in Mexico City, Uber drivers took us everywhere. One highlight was to Frida Kahlo's bright Blue House studio and gallery in the Coyoacán artists' quarter. Kahlo is one of Mexico's best-known painters, feminists, and revolutionaries. Although disabled by polio as a child, she was a brilliant eighteen-year-old student bound for medical school when a bus hit her, which caused lifelong pain and medical problems. She is best known for her colorful self-portraits, often shown with a monkey that art historians believe represented children she was unable to bear, having lost one in a miscarriage. Her paintings today are worth millions of dollars, one selling in 2020 by Christie's for $8 million. Not to be outdone, the Palacio Nacional Museo exhibits dramatic historic murals by Diego Rivera that show the passion and fight for equality by Mexican workers and peasants.

Our calendar showed it was December 24. Even though we are not Catholic, when in Mexico, you do as they do—attend mass at Our Lady of Guadalupe Cathedral on Christmas Eve. What a unique and memorable experience for two American Protestants. Inside the hushed cathedral there were no Christmas carols, no lighting of candles, no Christmas wreaths, no choir singing "Away in the Manger"—just a six-foot-long slumbering baby Jesus resting in a rustic wooden cradle near the altar. Cobalt-blue and white lights streamed down on him as his pious young mother Mary bowed her head in prayer. Beggars and elderly and homeless people drifted in and out of the cathedral, along with families dressed in their finest attire, kneeling, making the sign of the cross, and praying. A young handsome priest in a long, white robe spoke Spanish or Latin, intoning in such a low monotone I was not sure if anyone could hear or understand him. The atmosphere was quiet and solemn, and echoes bounced off the stone walls. No singing of "Silent Night, Holy Night," just feelings of Feliz Navidad as we headed out to the streets and found a Baskin Robbins ice cream shop packed with friendly Mexican families. We wished them Feliz Navidad and ordered our jamoca almond fudge ice cream on Christmas Eve.

CHAPTER 20

Fixing What's Wrong

A few weeks after returning from Mexico City, I continued my most important job I ever had as an elected Colorado State Representative. My friend Senator Cheri Jahn had mentored me to keep me out of trouble. For example, she explained the protocol regarding legislative functions and meetings in the Capitol: "If you're early for the meeting, you're on time; if you're on time, you're late; if you're late, you're toast." So I had arrived early at 8:55 a.m. for the Chief Justice of the Colorado Supreme Court to swear me in on January 7, 2009. I began to love the daily color guard, the Pledge of Allegiance, the morning prayer, and musicians that opened each morning's session. I looked forward to the first committee reading of bills when the public comes in to testify. Members of the Democratic caucus became my best and loyal friends. And I even made friends with conservative and fundamentalist Republicans like the rancher who, with a little persuasion and courtesy, said he would consider voting for my physical therapist licensing bill. I'll never forget him with a silver crew cut, cowboy hat, western boots and with a large, gold Christian cross attached to an American flag on his lapel.

I was sponsoring this bill requiring physical therapists to be licensed, and I was very surprised that it was not already a law. "I hate laws and more laws including yours," he blurted out to me. But when I discovered that his own son was a physical therapist, I took the time to discuss with him why the licensing of physical therapists was good for their credibility, their income, their future, and certainly for public safety. When the final vote came, I looked at the House vote electronic board, which shows a vote for yes in green, and a vote for no in red. Guess what: he had pressed the green button. A little courtesy, listening, and personal attention go a long way in Colorado politics. I was overjoyed to sponsor and help pass bills that improved the education, health, economy, and environment of our beloved Centennial State.

Many citizens have asked me just how does an idea or project become a law? There are many, many ways, and here are a few examples: 1) a state agency might request a new law; 2) a state representative or senator might have heard or read about a law or policy from another state or country; 3) a citizen might suggest to their state senator at a townhall meeting that, for example, there ought to be a law about safer clearance for bicyclists on Colorado highways; 4) a neighbor at a coffee shop recognizes a representative and asks for leadership in banning assault weapons; or 5) a legislator at a national legislative conference picks up a list of important laws passed by other states. There are national associations that collect and track all the bills and laws from fifty states and keep lists by subject for any elected official to consider on any given topic—agriculture, business, technology, labor, education, finance, judiciary, health, human services, local government, state veterans and military affairs, transportation, and others.

In Colorado, for example, a state agency like the Department of Health Care Policy and Finance (HCPF) might want the legislature to pass a law that makes Medicaid more available and affordable for lower-income people. The director of HCPF would contact the Speaker of the House and the president of the Senate, get their opinions, and if the responses are positive the Speaker and the president would decide which legislators would best sponsor the bill in the House and the Senate. Then a legislative lawyer called a drafter would write the bill in legal language and ask the legislators for their approval. Once the draft is completed, the Speaker or president would assign it to the appropriate first committee like in this case to the Health and Human Services Committee.

I will briefly summarize how I was able to pass an important bill into law in 2009. Since the age of fifteen, I said if something is wrong, let's fix it, but never just by myself. I had read that insurance companies charged women more for private health insurance coverage than men. This seems wrong, and I will try to fix it—yes! I had read about a law passed in Massachusetts that required gender-fair premiums for individual health insurance coverage. Previously women were charged much more than men for individual health insurance coverage. Why? Because they might get pregnant. Really? Not all women get pregnant! This was an irrational reason to charge women more. The bill passed in Massachusetts, so why not Colorado? But some senior leaders in my caucus objected telling me that I can't fight the powerful insurance lobby, which would crucify me, and the bill would die in the first committee known as being Postponed Indefinitely. Undeterred, I took this idea to the Speaker of the House, to a Senator sponsor, and they supported the idea as I explained it. I immediately filed the idea/bill for consideration. Next I asked my fellow Democrats and some likely sympathetic Republicans if they would support the idea and if they wanted to be listed as co-sponsors. Many did.

Next my bill was assigned to the appropriate Health and Human Services Committee. I immediately met one-on-one with as many committee members as I could to try to gain their support or their opposition even before the first meeting. As the sponsor, I did not want any surprises from Democrats or Republicans over my most-cherished bill, so I anticipated all their questions and/or objections. It felt like I was pregnant and doing everything I could to protect this precious offspring. Then this committee of fifteen legislators gathered and the committee chair announced the public hearing was in session.

As the sponsor, I explained it and asked for comments and questions from the committee members. Then the chair invited comments and questions from the public citizens and lobbyists assembled in the committee room. Finally the chair asked for a voice vote by committee members on my bill. Since I had counted my likely votes before the official meeting, I was relieved my bill did pass its first test with a positive vote. There's an old saying in the legislature and in other endeavors that says: "Proper preparation prevents poor performance," and that was certainly true in my case.

Another old saying I used in the legislature was "Leave no stone unturned." I was getting paranoid, but my bill was so important I turned over every stone I could find. Where would opposition come from? How can I answer their concerns? Can I amend my bill in order to get their approval? Other good advice I learned early on was "Carry your bill, don't marry it." This means don't die if your bill fails; there will be many more opportunities for improving this bill and/or for sponsoring other bills.

This first process is called the First Reading of a Bill. When my important bill passed out of this first committee, it went next to the sixty-five House legislators for discussion and for answering questions. This process is called the Second Reading of Bills, and I met individually with as many colleagues as I could before the Second Reading voice vote. Next came the Third Reading, which would be a final recorded vote (green light for yes, red light for no) from the sixty-five House Representatives. Success. My bill passed, but now how does the Senate sponsor get it through the Senate? That is her responsibility. I trusted her 100% and the Senate did pass the bill. But it was not a law yet. I was getting tired. But having explained the major provisions to the governor much earlier (governors do not like surprises), I was confident he would sign my bill and he did. Gender-fair premiums were now the law in Colorado.

When President Obama signed the Patient Protection and Affordable Care Act in 2010 also known as the Affordable Care Act and Obama Care, individual health care gender-fair premiums were now the law of the entire land. As a footnote to my gender-fair health care premiums bill, I had done earlier research showing that men tend to neglect their health and actually cost insurers more than women in the long run. Neglecting their medical care means men tend to have higher incidences of heart attacks, diabetes, cancer, alcoholism, and obesity. Unfortunately, today in 2024 Donald Trump will try to negate the Affordable Care Act and replace it with what? He does not say. Millions of Americans without affordable, reliable care needing to buy private health insurance? Bad idea.

Most states have hundreds of bills introduced each year, which makes sponsoring bills very time consuming, requiring legislators to work many twelve-hour days, some weekends, and even holidays. An old political axiom is "legislating is like making sausage." This is false because there are recipes for sausage with specific ingredients and quick steps, whereas every year in Colorado legislating can takes twists, turns, upsets, drama, trauma, and sometimes 120 days a year.

Another important bill of which I was a Prime House Sponsor was the 2013 Colorado Civil Unions Bill. I believed it was wrong that in our state and country LGBTQs could not marry the one they love, inherit property, or win custody of their children. This certainly needed to be fixed. We needed a civil unions bill, which might set the course eventually for gay marriage. I set out to fix this wrong with House Bill 13-011 but not my myself.

The Colorado Civil Unions Law would ensure that gay, lesbian, bisexual, and transgender couples have rights similar to married couples. This bill enraged the far right, and many Republicans cried, "LGBTQs are immoral, sick pedophiles who prey on children. The state should never grant them the same rights as heterosexuals. This bill will destroy the moral fabric of our state. Pedophiles will roam our schools and recruit our children into this debased lifestyle." Apparently many so-called Christians had not read their Bible with Paul's letter to the Galatians: chapter 3:28, "All of you are one in Christ Jesus." We are all God's children, including LGBTQ persons.

With a narrow House and Senate Republican majority, I knew HB13-001 was vulnerable but doable if we Democrats played our cards right. We quickly activated our allies to lobby for the bill: ACLU, CEA, PFLAG, HRC, LWV, Colorado Women's Bar, AFL-CIO, Interfaith Alliance, ADL, and many more. We identified the few persuadable Republicans on the judiciary committee and showed them courtesy and personal attention to get the few votes needed. And the "coming out" of many Democratic legislators, including the highly respected Minority Leader of the House, Mark Ferrandino, and Senators Lucia Guzman and Patrick Steadman had proved that the vast majority of LGBTQs, like most heterosexuals, are intelligent, honest, and hardworking citizens. We, the sponsors of the bill, met individually with those who opposed it. When legislators in 2013 learned about our personal lives and how the bill would protect us, our property and our children, many fears and myths about LGBTQs had lifted.

On the day of the judiciary committee hearing about HB13-011, the hot steamy room in the Old Supreme Court Chamber was packed with 250 parents, journalists, presidents of nonprofits, CEOs, and clergy of Christian, Jewish, and Muslim congregations that were for or against the bill. My homework assignment had been to have coffee with two Republican women who could be the two yes votes and were more amenable to the bill than the men. The hearing started at 1:30 p.m., lasted until 10:00 p.m., and the vote was seven yes and four no. So far so good.

After the judiciary committee vote, we later moved the bill to the dreaded appropriations committee where several penny-pinching members and opponents of the bill said that we couldn't afford it. The fiscal analyst, however, had estimated that the proposed law would cost the state $4,500 out of a $28-billion budget. Was this too much to pay for full equality? When the bill went to the entire House for a vote among the sixty-five representatives, it passed with fairly strong support, 38–27. From the House, the next goal was passage by the Senate—stodgy, doddering senators who woke up from their naps to listen to the pros and cons of this legislation. (We joked about Senators because the origin of the word *senator* comes from the Latin *senex*, related to *senile*.)

In lobbying for this bill, I remembered what Anne Lamott wrote: "In order to get anything done, you need to plod along, one step at a time, or 'just go one bird by one bird.'" So with each representative and senator, we did go personally to each of them. This bird-by-bird approach is also effective while reaching across the aisle or better yet, not just reaching, but getting up out of your seat and walking across the aisle to speak privately with each elected official.

As a result, a majority of senators voted 20–15 for the Colorado Civil Unions Law of 2013. OMG, we did it! Three weeks later, brass bands played "God Bless America," "When the Saints Go Marching In," "I Am What I Am," and "The Best of Times Is Now" in the lobby of the Colorado History Museum. Purple balloons, red-white-and-blue banners, and thousands of LGBTQs wearing rainbow-colored T-shirts waved and cheered from the four marble balconies. Hundreds of their friends, parents, elected officials, ministers, journalists, and police officers waited patiently for Governor John Hickenlooper who was seated on the stage to sign the bill with his gold Cross pen. Finally civil unions for LGBTQ people in Colorado was the law of the land.

The Colorado Civil Unions law was not gay marriage, but it provided case law and momentum for future gay marriage in America. The historic struggle for gay marriage formally started in 2003 when the Massachusetts Supreme Court ruled that banning gay marriage was unconstitutional. From 2003 to 2015, there were numerous state court rulings, direct popular votes, and federal court rulings to produce sufficient case law for the US Supreme Court on June 26, 2015, to declare by a 5–4 vote that gay marriage was the law of the land. I remembered since the age of fifteen that when something is wrong, we will fix it. Forbidding gay people who love each other to marry was wrong, wrong, wrong, and we fixed it.

After sharing my personal story of growing up gay but not knowing how to manage my life when homosexuality was forbidden, I've come to regret the pain and suffering I caused my parents, my former husband, and my two daughters. I have remorse for lying about who I was and masquerading as heterosexual throughout my professional career. Passing as straight, however, was necessary back then and maybe today to some degree to retain jobs when employees are fired for being gay.

After the 2015 Supreme Court ruling legalizing gay marriage, and many state laws prohibiting discrimination against LGBTQ people in employment, housing, and public accommodations, I'm thankful that new generations of LGBTQs can live with less hate, less fear, and less disdain than I did. But of course, if I'd known I was gay, I would not have married and borne two beautiful daughters, Mary and Annie, who are the loves of my life. Nor would I be the bragging grandmother of three granddaughters.

Fear and hatred of LGBTQs still encourages crime and violence against us. On June 12, 2016, hundreds of LGBTQs were dancing under a warm, starry night at the gay Pulse Nightclub in Orlando, Florida, when an angry gunman barged into the club, massacred forty-nine innocent people, and seriously injured fifty-eight others. Omar Mateen died in a shootout with police; his reason for the killings was that he saw a gay couple kissing. It's hard to know where we LGBTQs and others are safe now: schools, shopping centers, supermarkets, parks, parades, churches, and synagogues? Any public place?

I live in the state with the latest hate crime against LGBTQs—Colorado Springs, Colorado. On November 20, 2022, at the Club Q Nightclub an armed psychotic gunman entered the club with weapons and shot several innocent people who were out to enjoy a night with friends. The shooter killed five and injured nineteen others. The bartender died a hero while yelling to patrons to get down and take cover. The gunman, Anderson Lee Aldrich wearing military fatigues, was shot and captured by several heroic club members including a visiting military veteran. Aldrich is pleading innocent by reason of insanity.

As an elected state representative, I identified five other conditions that also were wrong and needed to be fixed with legal and financial support. These are in addition to the unfair individual health insurance premiums women were forced to pay, and we fixed this injustice with my bill as described earlier. Also several other legislators and I had fixed discrimination against LGBTQ couples with the civil unions law which led to gay marriage. I learned of other problems that needed fixing: abuse of elders, bullying of students, denying in-state college tuition to high-achieving immigrant students who had lived most of their lives in the US, denying low-income children the early childhood education they needed to succeed, and failing to provide services for persons living with intellectual and developmental disabilities (IDD). Something's wrong. Let's fix all of these. Where do I learn about these problems? I read the local and national papers including the sports news; I listen to local, state, and national news; I listen to friends, neighbors, and church members; I attend public hearings about local and state controversies. In other words, I keep my ears and eyes open, which anyone must do if they ever aspire to elected office.

Regarding the problem of elder abuse, I had heard that my Jefferson County, Colorado, had set up an elder abuse office, and I believed our entire state should have an elder abuse reporting law. I learned about elderly persons being financially, physically, and sexually abused, and having their life savings stolen by unscrupulous family members, bankers, or lawyers. I realized that anyone who knew about these crimes should be legally required to report these abusers to social services and/or to law enforcement just as all people are required to report suspected child abuse. Elder/senior citizens should receive the protection and compensation they deserve. To address these problems, a senator and I sponsored a bill to require this mandatory reporting of elder abuse, and it passed in 2015 with the support of 100 percent of both the Senate and the House of Representatives. Rarely does any bill pass with 100% of the legislature.

Fixing What's Wrong

Next I learned in the news about students who were hazing, bullying, ridiculing, and harassing other students, especially LGBTQ, disabled, Indigenous, Black, Hispanic, and ethnic students. A senator and I sponsored a bill requiring teachers to attend semi-annual in-service trainings to learn how to prevent and intervene with such hurtful behavior. Such bullying often results in absenteeism, anxiety, depression, low achievement, and even suicide. This bill hardly eliminated such hurtful behavior, but it has greatly reduced it. I am grateful for all our teachers and administrators who have reduced the incidence of bullying, but sadly, today in 2024, we citizens hear more about school shootings than we do about bullying. But often the shooter has been a victim of bullying at some time in his life. Curious: Why have there been no female shooters in schools?

I sponsored another bill with a senator that would allow undocumented, high-achieving Colorado high school graduates to attend Colorado colleges at the in-state tuition rate. These students are called Dreamers who, even though they are not "legal," when they graduate from college they are well educated, employable, and become strong contributors to society. Even with Republican opposition, this law did pass in our legislature by a very narrow margin.

And fourth, another bill I sponsored provided additional funding for low-income children to have more preschool education. I had read about thousands of parents wanting preschool for their young children but not being able to afford public or private preschools. Research shows children with preschool education are much better prepared for success in K–12, college, and life. In numerous polls, Colorado voters approved of universal preschool for all Colorado four-year-olds regardless of their parents' income, and Governor Polis signed a bill in 2022 for these children. What a strong life-changing investment for $35,000,000. I'm thinking about all children reading proficiently by third grade, which sets them on a path for success in life. Children not proficient in reading after grade 3 are at risk for the rest of their lives.

Another bill I sponsored came from a friend who is a lobbyist for the intellectually and developmentally disabled (IDD) population. He asked me if I would co-sponsor a bill in 2015 ending the wait list for services for children and adults with IDD. IDD includes all forms of physical and mental handicaps such as visually impaired, deaf, Down's syndrome, autism, low IQ, cystic fibrosis, and many other disabilities. This was a high moral imperative for me. I explained the bill in the first House Committee, then on Second Reading to the entire House, and finally to the House on Third Reading saying, "These persons, through no fault of their own were born with physical and cognitive disabilities which put them at risk when they are unable to depend on a safe home, food, clothing, health care, schooling, or a job. Therefore, it's time to end this wait list for services for our most vulnerable citizens." For decades, adults with IDD were not able to meet their most basic needs; children with IDD term out of public-school IDD services at age twenty-one. Another complication for persons with IDD is that they are most often cared for by elderly parents and siblings who won't be able to sustain this care indefinitely.

With a state budget topping $30 billion in 2015, surely Colorado could support these IDD person's basic needs. This bill passed but with far less funding than needed. We didn't end the wait list for services, but every year the list got shorter with more financing. As a legislator I saw many things that were wrong that I could not entirely fix, but I believe that my fellow legislators and I did reduce the severity of these problems. In 2021 the legislature did make a significant investment in ending the wait list, but from 1920 to 2021, thousands of IDD citizens barely survived only due to the housing, food, medical care and financial resources from their families and friends.

Serving in the legislature actually made me feel like royalty, being treated with such immediate and gracious attention by house lawyers who drafted bills, by capitol security, the state patrol, and registered lobbyists. Anything I needed was provided immediately. For example, during a blinding snowstorm at 1:00 a.m. my car wouldn't start. I called the state patrol, and within three minutes an officer arrived in the parking lot with jumper cables, and I was on my way home. Once I asked a bill drafter (a lawyer) in 2012 to compose a proclamation honoring the fortieth anniversary of Title IX. She asked how soon I wanted this, and I said two days would be okay. Within three hours, the proclamation was on my desk complete with all the detailed progress that Title IX had brought over the past forty years.

"Evil lobbyists" is a misnomer because only one of over one thousand Colorado registered lobbyists ever made a threatening statement to me in order to get me to vote for his bill. The other 999 lobbyists took immediate action to answer any question or to solve any problem, even when I called them at midnight or at 5:00 a.m. I received tremendous assistance from the lobbyists representing the Colorado Education Association, the District Attorneys Association, the Colorado Women's Bar Association, the Colorado Medical Society, the Greater Denver Ministerial Alliance, AARP, the Chambers of Commerce, and the AFL-CIO to name a few. One of those lobbyists is a friend for life: Mr. Ed Bowditch lobbied for the Jefferson County, Colorado School Board and owns property in my home state of Maine. Along with actual legislative business, Ed and I enjoyed organizing the informal "New England Caucus" with Sen. Joann Ginal and Lt. Gov. Donna Lynne, both from New Hampshire. We shared "important" news to us such as the annual lobster catch in Maine and the return of bald eagles in Maine's Acadia National Park.

Beyond the capitol, we legislators took outside educational investigative trips. One of my favorite excursions and the most unusual was when I went to prison at the storied 1871 Old Territorial Correctional Facility near Canon City, Colorado. Located on dry, dusty clay with tumbleweeds and rattlesnakes, it's surrounded by black, twelve-foot-high steel fences with Do Not Enter signs and topped by five feet of razor wire. Years ago, even Billie the Kid was imprisoned there. Adobe walls as wide as barrels separate various wings of the prison.

I served as chair of the Correctional Industries Advisory Board. This Colorado Department of Corrections administers job training for well-behaving male and female inmates—programs such as dog trainer, fire fighter, fish hatchery technician, chef, appliance and auto repair technician, computer technician, graphic artist, dairy farmer, wild horse trainer, and forty other marketable skills needed in the current job market. Providing offenders with job training affords them the opportunity to be employed when they return to civilian society. Meanwhile, juvenile offenders' prisons give young people under eighteen a chance to earn a GED and/or college credits while receiving psychological and physical health care.

But certain sections of the prison system also contain great sorrows and despair. I was heartbroken to see children running and crying for joy to hug and kiss their drug-dealer mothers or to their fathers imprisoned for homicide. The solitary confinement/death row prisoners are granted only one hour per day in the gym or outside on the basketball court. I saw in the death chamber a ten-foot-long leather bench with thick, black straps and metal chains that would immobilize the convict before the lethal injection. I voted to repeal the death penalty in Colorado in 2020 because it had become government approved and sanctioned murder. Twenty-seven states still retain the death penalty in 2024.

I did learn how our prisons provide every opportunity for offenders to create a new life with programs such as high school and college education; medical, dental, and psychological care; alcohol and drug support groups; and even access to defense attorneys to appeal their sentences. Many offenders who took advantage of these programs succeeded in re-entering civilian life. However, despite some of the best services not even available to law-abiding citizens, the Colorado recidivism rate still hovers around 50 percent.

CHAPTER 21
It Appears Perfect

"Everything must be perfectly wonderful in the capitol!" several constituents told me. Not always. I experienced downsides serving in the legislature, such as twelve-hour meetings in hot, humid basement rooms; navigating the state capitol's icy, stone steps in high heels with sleet pelting my face; working hours of seven a.m. to eleven p.m.; Diet Coke and power bars for lunch; dry cardboard pizza and salty Cheetos for dinner; late-night filibusters until 1:30 a.m., used by opponents to kill a bill; and long-winded legislators who would pontificate ad nauseam at the well of the House chamber hoping to see themselves on television.

Despite these challenges, I strongly encourage anyone with a passion for justice, opportunity, and equality to stand up and run for elective office. You too can make a difference. You too can fix things when you see something is wrong. I always recommend candidate and campaign boot camps such as Emerge America for women or in Colorado Women Uprising. The Wellstone Academy trains both men and women. If you're not experienced in public speaking, I suggest taking the Toast Masters training. And find a mentor to learn the details of campaigning. Unfortunately no one encouraged me to run and no one formally mentored me, but I saw and listened to female elected officials whom I studied very carefully—their apparel, their speaking, their writing, and their interactions with citizens. Lesson learned: If I or any intelligent person knows someone who would be an effective elected official, speak up and encourage them to learn how to do this.

Serving in the Colorado House of Representatives for six years as the Honorable Sue Schafer was the greatest honor of my life. I highly recommend public service to anyone with a passion for good government. As of 2024, I still contribute to building the Democrats' pipeline by mentoring people aspiring to public office. Of course, I'll be mentoring my daughters and grand-daughters as future state representatives should their interests and abilities lead them to such a position. And the future is female.

In 2016 I retired from the House of Representatives which called for celebrating. As a history and geography buff, I desperately wanted to visit southeast Asia. So Barb and I took an exotic trip to the ancient kingdoms of Thailand, Laos, Cambodia, and Vietnam. First, Thailand. What can one say about this historic kingdom of coasts, plains, rain forests, and forested mountains? Thailand is like a huge rice paddy interrupted by the sprawling metropolis of Bangkok. Between the South China Sea and the Bay of Bengal are 68 million people whose ancestors migrated from China down the Mekong River to this area known as Thailand. Every city, town, village, office, and home has a Buddha statue in it; 95 percent of Thais are Buddhists. My first lesson in Thailand and southeast Asia was learning how to greet locals in the traditional way by pressing my hands together upright and bowing my head meaning, "the spirit in me greets the spirit in you" or "*namaste.*"

A local Bangkok woman invited us for lunch at her home on the banks of the Noi Canal where we cooked red curry to eat with sticky fried rice and spiced pork. I noticed in her home numerous photographs of her ancestors on a wall displayed with offerings of oranges and candies. The Thais pray for the spirits of their ancestors, who they believe to still be "alive," to inspire and guide them. In Bangkok I admired the Emerald Buddha, a sacred object carved from a single jade stone now in the Royal Chapel of the Grand Palace. This Buddha, which is about two feet tall and weighs three pounds was discovered in an ancient temple in 1434 and has been preserved for six hundred years. It's adorned with thin, gold shawls and is surrounded by yellow lilies, pink candles, and baskets for donations, all with the scent of jasmine incense. We waited in a long line of children and adults to honor and pray to this beloved Buddha.

I was afraid in Bangkok with thousands of loud motorcycles, buses, scooters, bicycles, and three-wheeled conveyances called *tuk tuks* that made crossing a street a death wish. On the streets I smelled wet markets selling bats and rats but dared not to sample any of them. My Thai friend encouraged me to "just try" some exotic delicacies like shark fins with scallop broth, chicken feet with cucumber pickles, sautéed chili paste on cuttlefish heads, and French-fried tarantulas. Yum! The tarantula legs tasted like French fries, but I could not eat the bellies, which were slimy but full of healthy protein. No, thank you.

We saw Bangkok people living in shanties along the canals, but most of them live in apartments. We saw the super-rich living in large homes with swimming pools and tennis courts in the suburbs. Millions of Thais are farmers and fishermen. One evening we took a dinner cruise on the Chao Phraya River which flows through the city. Viewing upscale Bangkok by night was quite the sight. We passed under gold-illuminated bridges with luxury stores located on the banks of the river. We decided this area of Bangkok must be therapy for the ultra-wealthy: Gucci, Chanel, Cartier, Prada, Versace, Rolex,

Lexus, the Four Seasons, and the Ritz-Carlton. Nice to look at, but our neighborhood and accommodations were perfectly matched to our budgets.

Next we flew into Laos and were surrounded by steep green mountains and views of thirty golden temples. We walked along the mighty Mekong River and heard local people ferrying their goods across channels to their homes and markets. What are those "night markets" I've heard about? They were fifty outdoor tents in towns and cities starting at sundown a few nights a week covered with strings of white lights and stalls selling great "bargains"—everything from leather goods, carpets, jewelry, shoes, dresses, bathing suits, fruit smoothies, Lao sausages, crispy rice salad, and homemade moonshine. And lucky me! I found a grand bargain: a rose-colored Rolex Oyster watch for only 328,000 Lao kip ($40.00), which the sixteen-year-old salesgirl assured me was not a knockoff but an authentic Rolex. It seemed too good to be true, but I wore it everywhere until its untimely death after two years.

On another day in Laos we cruised along the Mekong River and explored a cave buried under a steep cliff where Hmong people hid for three months in 1972 from the Vietnamese War attacks. The only problem was that in order to climb the cliff to the cave, we first had to cross the river on a narrow, swinging, bamboo footbridge that looked like a tightrope. No way! We are not the tightrope artists Wallendas. I didn't want to fall in a river where there are alligators. But gathering our courage, we very timidly did it. Once inside the dark, humid cave there were buddhas of every size with small pieces of fruit and candy on their laps donated by other climbers.

Exiting the cave we had to descend and take that swinging tightrope back again to reach the shore. I can't do it! Luckily I was inspired by looking across the river and saw water buffalo mothers

It Appears Perfect

and their calves grazing on the grassy shore. And we were also blessed to see at close range Asian elephant mothers and calves playing and spraying cool water at each other. FYI, Asian elephants are known for their small rectangular ears, unlike African elephants that have the big floppy ears.

We experienced a memorable event helping to cook a Lao dinner at the home of a matriarchal family: a sixty-five-year-old grandmother, her thirty-five-year-old Olympic badminton star daughter, and her twenty-one-year-old college student granddaughter majoring in environmental science. We stirred the fried rice, spicy pork, and green vegetables, but truth be told, these ladies did most of the cooking and we did most of the eating. Then without warning, the glamorous eighteen-year-old granddaughter jumped up with her iPod and cried, "Let's dance!" Waltzes, country, disco, and even some hip-hop filled the air. We twirled around the small upstairs apartment and were given cloth bracelets signifying a prayer for our health and good fortune. The next morning, we learned how to pray Buddhist style when we visited a young bald monk dressed in an orange garment. In a small monastery, he showed us how to sit while bowing our heads and whispering, "*Namaste*." I learned that monks spend a lifetime seeking enlightenment through the practice of meditation, morality, and wisdom. No small order. Hope it's not too late for me.

I had mixed feelings about visiting Cambodia whose history included some of the best and some of the worst in the world. The worst is the Cambodian Genocide when the dictator Pol Pot in 1972–1974 murdered two million doctors, nurses, teachers, journalists, musicians, and other intellectuals who were loyal to the king and would not support Pol Pot's dream of agrarian communism. We visited the "killing fields," where thousands of skulls and human bones were reverently displayed in cemeteries and in temples. One graveyard was the saddest of all, filled with millions of tiny children's skeletons and bones. There were other cruel dictators like Stalin and Hitler in modern history but few as evil and depraved as Pol Pot who tortured and executed his own people—1.5 million of them.

On the brighter side, our Cambodian visit to a tarantula farm (yes, they raise tarantulas in Asia) was actually a joyous occasion. We were to locate black tarantulas in glossy webs in the field where a pretty young farmer wearing silver leggings, bright-red lipstick, and Ray Bans trapped them and snipped off their stingers. "Wouldn't you all like to have a cute, hairy, six-inch tarantula crawl up your arm?" she asked.

"Okay . . . I would . . . I am woman!" I stuttered hesitantly. Most of the macho men in our group were too afraid to have a friendly tarantula crawl on their bodies, so we women rose to the occasion. Asians eat all kinds of insects so the farmer sautéed these spiders in a steel wok with olive oil and garlic and offered us a snack. I could eat only the crispy, fuzzy legs, which tasted like French fries. Yum! I posted on Facebook (FB) the photo of the five-inch-long tarantula crawling up my arm and 200 FB friends said they did not believe this. But I had proof with fifteen other tourists in my group witnessing this occasion. On another occasion I snacked on caterpillars and grasshoppers, but I won't make insects part of my regular diet. Why travel the world if you don't try different things?

As a history and geography buff, I was curious about a center in Phenom Penh that raises and trains African giant rats (called hero rats), which can detect incendiary unexploded devices (IUDs). The rats, which are tan and the size of a domestic cat weigh about twelve pounds. You can even snuggle with them because they, like cats, are very friendly. The American military left thousands of IUDs on roads and fields after the war ended and intentionally dropped unused bombs and missiles all over Cambodia. The US wanted to save the cost of carrying the IUDs back to the US. Thousands of acres of jungles, gardens, and rain forests were burned and destroyed, but worse, these IUDs have killed and maimed thousands of adults and children during the last fifty years, including farmers gathering their crops and children riding bicycles on trails.

The hero rats are trained in a twenty-foot-by-twenty-foot sandbox, but out in a field they can clear an area the size of a tennis court in a few hours. A human doing the same work would take at least eight hours. In the field they're on a leash connected to men in a nearby truck. When a rat smells the pungent IED gunpowder on a road or in a field, it scratches the location, which sends a signal that there's an IUD on that spot. The rat is not heavy enough to detonate the device, which allows men in a truck to pull the rat back in and then explode the landmine. It's estimated that these hero rats are responsible for saving over 60,000 human lives. See **www.apopo.org** for other inspiring stories. Today in 2024 a hero rat named Carolina has even detected early TB infections in people which can save their lives. (I'm not making this up.) In 2020, a hero rat named Magawa won the International Gold Medal Award for Animal Bravery and Accomplishment for detecting approximately one hundred IUDs and potentially saving one hundred or more human lives. Magawa died at age eight, a life well-lived. I now sponsor one hero rat in Cambodia for $99.00 per year. When I informed my family and friends that I'd adopted a giant African rat, they worried about it running around my house and vowed they would never visit me again. And this rat like a cat would not hurt anyone unless provoked.

I was very excited to view the temples of Angkor Wat, a holy city in Cambodia that is a UNESCO World Heritage Site. It is considered the largest religious structure in the world that sprawls across ninety-six square miles. Brilliant scientists, engineers, artists, and sculptors have spent 1,000 years building and rebuilding five huge sandstone temples adorned with the smiling faces of brave male warriors, beautiful female deities, and sacred elephants. Even though the temples were built by and for Hindus and Buddhists, any believer from any faith today feels welcome on this peaceful, sacred ground. I witnessed pre-wedding photographing of brides and grooms, and Buddhist monks in orange robes sitting with visitors while blowing incense on them for a blessing. After all these excursions, I was hungry for a Cambodian feast of fish amok, a steamed coconut fish wrapped in banana leaves or Khmer noodles with Angkor beer.

I have been fascinated for fifty years with the Socialist Republic of Vietnam having experienced the violence, outrage and pain during the American-Vietnamese war from 1966–1975. I needed to discover what Vietnam had become after it won the war. I found it necessary to review the history of those tumultuous years of pain and American casualties that tore American society apart. The US government had declared it needed to save South Vietnam from becoming a Communist country. "If South Vietnam falls to Communism, there will be a domino effect, tipping the entire Asian continent to Communism. We must save South Vietnam from the Communists!" insisted Presidents Johnson, Nixon, and military leaders. But the United States was seriously unprepared to wage a guerrilla war in humid rain forests with tangled vines, dense bamboo trees, giant lizards, poisonous dart frogs, spiders, ticks, boa constrictors, green anacondas, and enemy combatants concealed in the jungles. The US military also underestimated the determination and military force of the Viet Cong Communists patrolling South Vietnam.

During those war years, my husband, Don, was based on an aircraft carrier situated in the South China Sea. I prayed for his safe return and often didn't know if he was dead or alive. I lost two dear colleagues who were serving their country and who became part of the 58,000 Americans who sacrificed their lives in a losing war. By 1975 the ultimate "strategy" turned out to be "declare victory and leave," said President Johnson. So in 2019, I decided it was past time to visit Vietnam where the major industries are commercial fishing and the production of rice, rubber, and coffee. Surprisingly, Vietnam ranks second in the world behind Brazil as the largest exporter of coffee beans. In 2018 Brazil exported 2,592,000 metric tons of coffee beans per year followed by Vietnam exporting 1,650,000 metric tons. And there's nothing better than a tall, chilled Vietnamese drip coffee made with sweetened condensed milk with a hint of hazelnut.

Arriving in Saigon as the locals prefer to call it instead of its legal name, Ho Chi Minh City, we walked around admiring manicured gardens, Buddhist temples, handicraft shops, and food markets selling dog meat. Fellow tourists said we should rent scooters to see this energetic city of ten million people up close and personal. But we decided this was an invitation to die as we witnessed rickshaws, bicycles, motorcycles, taxis, buses, BMWs, and Mercedes speeding along, all honking horns, competing for spaces, and daring to edge each other out. Plus, we'd been invited to visit the mother of a Denver friend, Vivian Tran in Saigon, but we needed to hire a translator because the Tran family spoke no English, and we spoke no Vietnamese. Our tour guide found a handsome young college student who spoke almost perfect English and joined us for tea, coffee, and chocolate cakes at Mrs. Tran's duplex in the heart of bustling Saigon.

We were honored to meet local people and see and hear how they live. Mrs. Tran had sold groceries for thirty years on the sidewalk in front of her duplex. It had white marble floors and shelves filled with small marble buddhas, orange lilies, and pink bougainvilleas. The air smelled sweet from the jasmine incense wafting lazily from one corner of the living room. But the center of attraction in her home was her son's 2018 shiny silver and red Honda CTX motorcycle. It was parked in the living room because it was too valuable to be left out on the sidewalk. Her son used it for fun, and his day job was driving for Uber, which was quite a challenge considering traffic jams on city streets and massive bridge delays. He explained that driving for Uber was quite lucrative because most residents in Vietnam could not afford to own a car.

Saigon has many curiosities including ordinary apartments that during the war housed bazookas, spears, revolvers, bayonets, machetes, and assault rifles. There were trap doors in there so soldiers could climb down a ladder and hide underneath these normal-looking buildings until they could burst out and kill enemy combatants. As an amateur gourmet, I was happy to sample the local Saigon food. The menu included my choice of spiced pork on thick noodles, braised beef on rice noodles, shrimp salad, stir-fried water spinach, the national dish of pho (a rice-noodle soup filled with meat), dumplings, green vegetables, ginger, and charred onions. Add a side of slaw and a Vietnamese 333 Beer, and I had a healthy feast.

On our last Saturday mid-December night in Saigon, the Vietnamese locals started celebrating the 2020 Lunar New Year three weeks in advance. Lucky us. The Saigon City Center cobblestone plaza was alive with rock bands, firecrackers, red and gold flags, balloons, games, and food trucks for thousands of people to enjoy. Grandparents with grandbabies, parents with toddlers, lovers young and old, gay and straight, dancing teenagers—the whole world was anticipating the Year of the Rat, which would officially begin on January 25, 2020. On December 29, 2019, we bid adieu to this fabulous, friendly country and flew from Saigon/Ho Chi Minh City to Tokyo, to Denver in time to celebrate New Year's Eve in the US. Two New Year's celebrations!

The Year of the Rat had already brought us a safe journey, good luck, good fortune, and new friends. Little did we know in the Year of the Rat 2020, we would be celebrating the end of the four miserable years of Donald Trump and the beginning terms of President Joseph Biden and Vice President Kamala Harris. Thank God for the Year of the Rat.

CHAPTER 22

The Four-Year Nightmare

Serving in the Colorado legislature from 2009–2015, I encountered hundreds of elected officials, lobbyists, journalists, and citizens with passionate opinions and relentless determination to fight for their legislative goals. We had fiery and angry debates, but never did I experience sarcasm, insults, lying, bribing, and cruelty from a fellow elected official, the president of the United States, Donald J. Trump. I don't want to write about those incredibly chaotic and painful four years, but it is important for the historical record for readers to learn how the Trump era affected me, millions of average American citizens, and foreign allies alike. Every cruel thing he said or did crushed my soul but not my determination to oust him in 2020 and 2024.

With Trump's election in 2016, our nation, our allies, and of course I suffered through the worst president in American history, according to Tim Naftali in *The Atlantic,* January 19, 2021. Historians and political scientists rank James Buchanan, Warren G. Harding, and Andrew Johnson as some of the worst until Trump surpassed them all. Trump is the only US president who has been impeached twice. Buchanan supported white supremacy leading up to the Civil

War. Warren G. Harding's administration was replete with multiple scandals and massive corruption, and Andrew Johnson fought against the passage of the Fourteenth Amendment which guaranteed equal protection under the law for the newly emancipated enslaved people. In comparison, the best presidents such as Abraham Lincoln, George Washington, Franklin D. Roosevelt, and Theodore Roosevelt were not perfect, but rank high in achievements and positive leadership and low in failures and faults.

Early in his campaign, voters learned that Trump had bragged to others about sexually abusing women and paying off a pornography star to silence her about their affair. Brandy X. Lee, MD, a psychiatrist at Yale University and an international expert on violence along with thirty other healthcare professionals wrote that they opposed Trump due to his dangerous mental condition. They believed that he had the real potential to become an even more dangerous threat to the safety of our nation and concluded that he is a malignant narcissist. I had trouble sleeping after Trump's election in 2016 after weathering his daily insults, scandals, sarcasm, and ridicule of national and international leaders.

To be fair, Trump did build on Obama's economy; the US became the world's most prosperous economy and 7 million Americans got jobs during his four years. Also unemployment among African Americans and Hispanics reached historic lows. However, during his wrecking-ball administration, every day I was shattered by his lies and wondered how our nation could survive four years of the unethical and crude things he said and did. Millions of Americans, our allies and I lived in psychic despair promulgated by the most powerful man in the world with his hand on the nuclear code.

For the record, I recall numerous hateful statements he made, each one causing a headache and piercing my soul. He called the

American free press the enemy of the people; he started trade wars with China; he used toxic slapstick such as making fun of disabled people and joking about buying Greenland, a sovereign nation. He derisively labeled small, struggling democracies like Ukraine as "shithole" countries. Trump called US Senator John McCain a "loser" who was actually a war hero surviving a Vietnamese POW camp for five years where he was tortured and even lost his hand.

Of course Trump was a draft dodger by claiming bone spurs and called US military veterans "losers" and "suckers." One sick announcement was that he could shoot someone on Fifth Avenue, New York City, and his cult of followers would still vote for him. He ripped 545 children from their Mexican parents who were deported to Mexico from the US border while their children as young as two were locked in cages in the US. Not to be outdone by her brutish husband, beauty queen wife Melania Trump, wearing a khaki denim jacket embroidered with "I Really Don't Care, Do U?" gazed at children in cages at the border.

On January 20, 2021, when Joseph R. Biden and Kamala D. Harris were inaugurated as president and vice president, Trump refused to accept his loss in the 2020 election and on January 6, 2021, he incited a mob of thousands of armed white supremacists, neo-Nazis, and anti-government militias to attack the United States Capitol. They broke windows, trashed and stole computers, defecated on marble floors, sprayed urine on walls and sculptures, threw beer cans from balconies, and killed five people, including one police officer. The damage almost destroyed the historic building. Not since the War of 1812 had our Capitol been so ferociously attacked. President Trump watched from his White House office. How he incited this insurrection earned him a shameful second impeachment. Trump as the commander in chief could have prevented this insurrection but instead sat idly by watching it on TV from the White House. What a loser, what a traitor.

Trump became the first and only president to be impeached twice, first for bribing the young forty-three-year-old Ukrainian president, Volodymyr Zelensky, and second for inciting the January 6, 2021, insurrection against the US Capitol and the United States democracy. Trump even had exhorted his vice president, Mike Pence, to invalidate the electoral count and declare Trump the president in January 2021. Pence refused to do this and became Trump's persona non grata. On January 6, 2021, Trump failed to stop the mob that put up gallows on the Capitol lawn with a huge HANG PENCE sign and noose on it. So much for Pence's adoring smiles, flattery, and lap-dog behavior trailing behind his master for four long years.

On election day November 6, 2020, I danced in the Denver streets with balloons and banners, and patriotic celebrations were held in many cities including a huge fireworks display in Wilmington, Delaware, Biden's hometown. This giant jubilation was notable for Vice President Elect Kamala Harris's historic affirmation: "I might be the first woman elected vice president, but I won't be the last." Huge cheers! It saddens me to think of what young Americans see and hear from Trump's Big Lie—that an election was "stolen" and thereby shattering young Americans' belief that America is the greatest democracy in the world.

Having survived this four-year nightmare, I celebrated the new Biden-Harris administration by building hope and resolution. Things are wrong, so let's fix them. I hope that with hard work we citizens will engage positively in electoral politics at all levels; that we will call out and fight racism, white supremacy, anti-Semitism, Islamophobia, and homophobia when we see it; that we will stop the new Jim Crow segregation voter suppression laws; that we will denounce QAnon and other conspiracy theories; that we will fight for policies to protect our land, air, and water; that we will work for all children to have a strong, quality education; that our communities of faith will marshal food, housing, and clothing for the poor and the homeless; and that we will practice human safety protocols like getting vaccinated, wearing masks, and practicing social distancing until the end of the Covid-19 pandemic. These goals are all possible if we are resolute to accomplish them. And as Vice President Kamala Harris declared, "If you are fortunate to have opportunity, it is your duty to make sure other people have those opportunities as well." And we Americans are blessed to have numerous opportunities.

CHAPTER 23

Finding Joy During the Four-Year Nightmare 2016–2020

Thankfully the four-year nightmare did not totally crush my spirit. I found joys such as our annual family reunion in Vail, Colorado, with relatives from Keller, TX; New York City; Pittsburgh; Seattle; Rochester, NY; and Colorado Springs. In 2016 there were two memorable occasions for me: using savvy, courage, and determination I aspired to win a seat to the July 2016 Democratic National Convention (DNC) in Philadelphia as a Colorado Hillary Clinton Delegate, and later that year Barb and I were able to travel to Norway.

But first, winning that Hillary Clinton Delegate seat meant competing with 150 other gay Colorado women at the state convention, the convention having quotas by gender, ethnicity, race, disability, and sexual orientation. I would have to explain what I would do as a Hillary Delegate from Colorado. Driving at 6:00 a.m. to the May 2016 Colorado Democratic State Convention in Loveland, Colorado, my friends Judith, Mary, and I traveled up in a blinding blizzard. When we arrived in Loveland, we were soaking wet with ice hanging on our heads, bodies, and clothes.

There were 150 lesbians aspiring to be a Hillary Delegate, but only two of us would be elected. In a caucus of these 150 lesbians, some candidates spoke of their vast experience such as being president of the Denver League of Women Voters or as a professor of political science at the University of Colorado, all very notable credentials. I, however, declared, "I will raise $10,000 for Hillary, I will recruit twenty-five volunteers to walk door-to-door for Hillary, and I will host three house parties for Hillary." The other highly qualified candidates had expounded on their credentials while my pragmatist pea brain determined that focusing on the tangible assets needed to elect Hillary was the best strategy. Would this work?

After the May 2016 state convention, a humorous incident in June 2016 occurred in Lakewood, Colorado, during the Clinton–Trump contest. I had stopped in a Safeway parking lot when a tall, bearded cowboy smoking a cigarette and wearing blue jeans and cowboy boots stopped me. He was wearing dark sunglasses, glaring at me, and pointing at the Clinton bumper sticker on my car. Then he asked, "*Hey*, where did you get *that*, that Clinton bumper sticker?"

Oh no, this man looks like a Trump supporter, I decided. Thinking he might rip it off, I cautiously squeaked, "Just down the street, sir, about six blocks. Er, why do you ask?"

"Because I want one!" he shouted.

We shook hands, and I gave him directions to the Hillary campaign office. I learned from him that he was a member of the AFL-CIO labor union. Lesson relearned: Don't make assumptions based on how people look.

Miraculously I did win the Hillary Clinton Delegate election with one other Colorado lesbian. I arrived in Philadelphia on July 25, 2016, for the DNC. Over 35,000 Democratic delegates cheered and sang for Hillary, while red, white, and blue flags fluttered over the Wells Fargo

Convention Center. We heard military bands playing Army, Navy, Marines, and Air Force fight songs, "God Bless America," and the national anthem. President Barack and First Lady Michelle Obama delivered soaring endorsements of Senator Clinton. We Colorado delegates were seated next to the mostly Black Louisiana delegates who entertained us by singing gospel songs, blaring trumpets, and waving purple and gold banners representing Louisiana State University.

Eating hot dogs, caramelized popcorn, pepperoni pizza, and jamoca almond fudge ice cream, we were blessed to hear Rev. Dr. William Barber II lift up prayers for Hillary after which all 35,000 of us stood up and shouted, "Amen!" We believed Hillary would be elected the forty-fifth president of the United States—by far the most intelligent, the most experienced, gracious, and most professional candidate. I will never recover from Senator Hillary Clinton's tragic loss to the worst president of the United States.

Now this worst president, the malignant narcissist, is threatening again to be elected in 2024. This is wrong. Let's fix it by campaigning for respectable candidates with no criminal records, no indictments, no malignant narcissism, and for people who respect and follow the rule of law.

In Philadelphia we delegates had a little time to visit the famous sites of this historic city. The Liberty Bell, the iconic symbol of American independence, weighs two thousand pounds, is made of copper, and stands four feet tall. Tourists from all over the world waited in long lines to be photographed with the symbol of the home and the brave. At Independence Hall, I was chilled seeing how small and crowded the room and furniture were where the framers of the Declaration of Independence and the Constitution debated and adopted these sacred documents. As of 1979, Independence Hall is now a UNESCO World Heritage Site.

As a history buff I aspired to visit the Philadelphia storied indoor Reading Terminal Farmers Market. Since 1893, farmers, ranchers, dairy men, butchers, chefs, cooks, weavers, and fishermen have brought their products to the market, which is situated on old railroad tracks. What a sight! Whatever you want or need is there: five towering food halls with Philly cheesesteaks; rows of bratwurst and pizza; trays of steaks, pork and lamb chops, chicken, salmon, oysters, crab; stacks of fresh produce; forty varieties of ice cream; clothing such as scarves, coats, dresses, slacks, beads, and boots; kegs of beer; shelves of whiskey, vodka, gin, and rum; and cameras. I had eaten Philly cheesesteaks before but nothing compared to an original Philly cheesesteak—sliced beef on a bun loaded with provolone cheese, caramelized onions, and Cheez Whiz. With all this shopping and eating at the Reading Market, we Democrats certainly did help the local economy.

Another joy during the 2016–2020 years was attending the annual Auburn Theological Seminary Lives of Commitment Awards breakfast at the Cipriani Events Center in New York City. I gain courage and strength hearing stories of great women like several honored recently, such as lesbian Jewish senior rabbi Sharon Kleinbaum, political activists Stacey Abrams and Chelsea Clinton, US Sen. Tammy Duckworth, Spelman College president Dr. Johnetta Cole, novelist Alice Walker, US Representative Lucy McBath, primatologist Dr. Jane Goodall, and many others.

Auburn Seminary, which is located at 475 Riverside Drive near Columbia University in New York City, doesn't ordain ministers; its mission is to "trouble the waters, and heal the world" and to provide professional development for interfaith leaders with multifaith and multiracial leadership development. Following the celebrated, fifteen-year powerful leadership of the Rev. Dr. Katherine Henderson, the Rev. Dr. Emma Jordan-Simpson, an inspired Black theologian, took the baton in 2021 as the new president of the Auburn Seminary at www.auburnseminary.org.

This seminary evolved from Harriet Tubman's courageous underground "railroad" from the Maryland plantations to Auburn, New York, where she helped enslaved people escape and get settled. Tubman donated part of her land and home to the Tubman Home for the Aged. She was a woman of historic moral courage and is believed to have rescued more than three hundred enslaved people at great risk to herself, all the while being chased by bounty hunters carrying guns, traps, and nooses.

In the current year, how thankful I am that my daughter Mary serves on the Seminary's Awards Committee, and my son-in-law Nate serves on the Seminary's Board of Directors. How gratifying it is to see this younger generation stepping into activism for alleviating racism, sexism, and homophobia, for fair immigration, for universal healthcare, for quality education, and for a sustainable planet on which to live. We all need to "trouble the waters"—rise up against injustice to heal the world.

Speaking of action to heal the world, on my international trips visiting with citizens from thirty-five countries as diverse as Botswana, Mexico, Australia, Israel, France, Canada, Greece, Norway, Cambodia, Thailand, Ecuador, Spain, Portugal, Argentina, and Brazil, I interacted with numerous citizens who showed me massive amounts of courtesy, respect, and love working for us all "to heal the world."

I was blessed in Rio de Janeiro, Brazil, recently to stand at the base of Christ the Redeemer, an Art-Deco UNESCO World Heritage Site and one of the Seven Wonders of the Modern World. This white concrete statue stands four stories high and weighs 635 metric tons. The best part at the Redeemer's base were the interfaith tourists—Muslims, Jews, Christians, Hindus, Buddhists, Pagans, and atheists admiring his outstretched arms conveying welcome, unity, and acceptance for all God's children. The Redeemer even invites weddings and baptisms under his base where we witnessed the baptism of a baby boy with his adoring family.

Not to be outdone by Brazil, Argentina's border with Brazil provides one of the Seven Wonders of the Natural World. The Iguazu International Waterfalls are the largest and widest falls in the world—larger than Niagara Falls in America and Victoria Falls on the border of Zambia and Zimbabwe. The Iguazu Falls number 275 and stretch east and west, north and south as far as the eye can see. For adventurous folks like Barb and me, we took a riverboat ride beneath one stretch of the less turbulent falls, getting soaking wet even with rain jackets and ponchos on.

In Buenos Aires, Argentina, I was inspired by the life of Eva "Evita" Duarte Perón (1919–1952) who is still considered the inspirational leader of Argentina. Evita saw that things were very wrong in Argentina when women were not allowed to vote. At her tomb I honored her courageous leadership in a patriarchal society that led the efforts for women to win the right to vote in 1947. And her memory is a blessing for me.

The great joy of travel helped me manage the four-year nightmare of Trump, of blazing wildfires, hurricanes, floods, and crucial Black Lives Matter protests. I mourned for the lives of over one million Americans as of April 2022 that the coronavirus pandemic claimed. During my quarantine of eighteen months, I lost access to my public library, travel to see my granddaughters in Texas and New York City, coffees and dining with old and new friends, book clubs, and tennis matches with colleagues—hardly great losses compared to the illnesses and deaths that one million Americans suffered. Thankfully I lost none of my family members or friends to the coronavirus, our mortgage was paid off, and we live on secure pensions. And I used considerable quiet time to write this memoir. I even did more home cooking, like Mama's red-hot chili, pumpkin bread with chocolate chips, broccoli and asparagus quiche, and baked chicken with mushroom soup and sherry spread over jasmine rice. Bon appétit.

In addition to the climate disasters and the Covid pandemic, I was deeply saddened by the murder of an African American man named George Floyd on May 25, 2020, in Minneapolis, Minnesota. He was suffocated by police officer Derek Chauvin who knelt and pressed on Floyd's neck for nine minutes, even while Floyd was gasping for air and crying, "I can't breathe." Protests against police brutality erupted across the country and the globe. American police forces say they are committed but struggling to reform their practices. We must stop the hate toward African Americans by working with the historic National Association for the Advancement of Colored People (NAACP), other civil rights groups, and communities of faith.

On a much happier note on August 26, 2020, I celebrated the one hundredth anniversary of the 19th Amendment to the US Constitution when women won the right to vote in 1920. I was stunned to realize my own grandmothers couldn't vote until 1920, which is rather recent history. I can imagine Grandmother Mary Daugherty Hosack in Pennsylvania and Grandmother Elizabeth Coleman Pierce in Nebraska fighting for the right to vote as Republican committee women.

CHAPTER 24

From Sunrise to Sunset

Now facing my sunset years, I do wonder if I've lived up to the benefits my four early cultures instilled in me. Did the New England coast teach me to be daring and courageous? Yes. I ran for and won an elected office. Did the wild Nebraskan prairie teach me to confront challenges with determination and grit? Yes. I gave birth and raised two healthy children. Did the abundant Pennsylvanian farmland teach me to be generous with my bounty? I could do better by donating more time and money to my Congregational Church UCC and to numerous other nonprofits. And did the rugged Rocky Mountains teach me to strive higher in nature and in life? Pretty well as I mentor young people so they can reach their highest goals. But I am certainly not finished, and I intend to keep going.

I am thankful for the gift of generational wealth that our parents won for many of us. Most Caucasian parents provided the means that enabled their offspring like me to earn college degrees and to buy homes, to work at good-paying full-time jobs that paid for pensions and healthcare. But thousands of Black, Hispanic, Asian, Indigenous, LGBTQ, and disabled babies were unable to achieve the American

Dream due to the entrenched racism and bias that persists to this day. This is wrong and I will continue to try to fix discrimination of any kind.

What are we who live now in 2024 leaving to our children, grandchildren, nieces, and nephews? Even though my grandchildren benefit from white privilege, they and millions of other children around the world are at risk as they face unsettled global economics, poverty, climate change, climate catastrophes, racism, sexism, anti-Semitism, Islamophobia, homophobia, war, animal cruelty, and pandemics. What will it take for all the children of all the people to be able to inherit the kinds of benefits our parents provided for us? How do we teach all the children to excel at school, work hard, save money, have a faith, obey the laws, get along with people, become a team member, be courteous, and respect everyone?

Looking back on our lives, my partner, Barb, and I did have to clear the hurdles of sexist counseling and sexual harassment in the pre-feminist era before 1970. For example, might Barb have become a medical doctor or Army general instead of being channeled into journalism and teaching? Might I have become a lawyer or a judge instead of being led into teaching? Despite the narrow career options, my education brought me great joy and pride as I helped to raise future generations. But I do still wonder if another career path might have proved more challenging and better suited to my abilities. It is certainly thanks to the feminist movement that today's girls and women have multiple career options, wherever their interests and abilities may lead.

However, severe and cruel barriers still do exist for girls and women. In some countries in Africa, Southeast Asia, and the Middle East, girls and women suffer genital mutilation, which consists of the partial or total removal of the clitoris and other genital organs for non-medical reasons. This is done without anesthesia causing violent pain and sometimes death. As of 2023, UNICEF estimates that 200 million girls in thirty-one countries have been subjected to this painful procedure. Other forms of hatred toward girls and women include rape, sexual assault, sex trafficking, forced pregnancy by making abortion illegal, and hiring and job discrimination. Such practices are used to keep girls and women across the world in their subservient and dangerous places. Let's fix all this for God's sake. As a grandmother of three young granddaughters, I wonder, *Where are the men, fathers, boyfriends, male CEOs, male medical doctors, Boy Scouts leaders, male NFL and NBA coaches to advocate for safety and respect for the women in their lives and for all women?* Men love cars, right? What if the AAA (American Automobile Association) led a campaign of We Respect Women? These powerful men could change the world for women, but they do nothing with their power to protect girls and women.

Collective action by groups working to fix these crimes include but are not limited to the American Civil Liberties Union (ACLU), the Anti-Defamation League (ADL), the Human Rights Campaign (HRC), Mothers Against Drunk Driving (MADD), NAACP, the National Organization for Women (NOW), Planned Parenthood, Southern Poverty Law Center, the United Nations Educational, Scientific and Cultural Organization (UNESCO), and the United Nations International Children's Emergency Fund (UNICEF). Join them, donate to them, volunteer, and work with them.

Over these past thirty years, Barb and I have thankfully achieved our goals, taken care of friends and family, compromised, danced, laughed, traveled the world, survived illnesses and accidents, rescued three dogs and two cats, and thankfully bought a midcentury modern home. We have mourned the deaths of our mothers and fathers, Barb's brother Jimmy Nash, and my brother-in-law Dr. Gary Phillips. Jimmy was a popular hairstylist known as the Denver Hairstylist to the Stars due to his styling hair and applying makeup for actors coming to perform in Denver's theatrical productions. Jimmy delighted clients and friends with his witty fashion advice, such as when I asked about the latest style in lesbian fashion, he quipped that the term "lesbian fashion" is an oxymoron. Right! He also stated regarding women's hair, "The higher the hair, the closer to God." Gary, my brother-in-law, survived violent whippings from his coal miner father but raised four successful children and became a professor and international motivational speaker pleading for the joyful classroom and the humane treatment of students.

Another joy in our sunset years is sharing new interests like raising a second Boston terrier puppy named Billie Jean after our twelve-year-old Boston terrier Patsy Cline passed away. Originally I hated dogs and never ever wanted to own one. But that changed when I first saw that tiny eight-week-old Patsy with her sweet face, which convinced me I was seeing the face of God. How could anyone but God create such a beautiful, lovable, perfect little angel? We enjoy birding, hiking, musicals, and book clubs, which inject novelty into our relationship. We also enjoy more concerts, films, operas, television, and lectures like the University of Denver Authors series, *Hamilton, Schindler's List, Les Misérables, Tosca, Carmen*, the Aspen Music Festival, *Fiddler on the Roof, La Cage aux Folles, Bohemian Rhapsody, Real Time With Bill Maher, Veep,* and my all-time favorite, *Schitt's Creek.*

Of course, we do have challenges: How much time do we spend together and apart? How do we take care of our aging bodies? What do our beloved friends, siblings, children, in-laws, grandchildren, and dogs need? We also must address how to spend our money: home improvements, travel, long-term care, division of assets, preparing to die, and planning our burials. We spent years planning our futures and, as a humorist once quipped, "Today is the tomorrow you dreamed about yesterday." But I don't dream about dying. Leo Tolstoy's character Ivan in *The Death of Ivan Ilyich* writhed in pain on his death bed and gasped: (Not exact quotes) "Hm, did I live as I should have lived? I earned the rank of Army colonel and ordered Russian soldiers to kill young men. I prosecuted criminals in court to earn a lot of money. I climbed the ladder of Russian high society. Now I wish I had worked for the poor." Maybe I should have done more for the poor, but as Edith Piaf crooned: "Je ne regrette rien." I regret nothing. And as an elder activist, I still have more time to help the poor.

As an activist in the 1950s and working for girls and women to be able to have competitive sports, I also worked for many other important causes. But I did nothing by myself. I addressed what was wrong and tried to fix the injustices with millions of other committed citizens. Each of us was and is like a drop of water wearing down boulders of injustice. When something is wrong, let's fix it. There is much injustice to be fixed, but determination, courage, intelligence, generosity, light, and love are always inspiring and supporting us.

From my fifteen-year-old activist age to now being an elder activist, I have the responsibility to safeguard my country's survival and to protect and preserve the health of the earth and its people. Rabbi Zalman Schachter-Shalomi in his book *From Age-ing to Sage-ing* credits Maggie Kuhn, an elder rights activist for identifying five roles for seniors: *mentors* to teach the young and the middle aged; *mediators* who work to resolve civil, racial, sexist, and intergenerational conflicts; *monitors* of public conflicts who serve as watchdogs of local, state, and national policy; *mobilizers* of social change and getting politically active; and especially, *motivators* of society who urge people away from self-interest toward generosity and the common good. We senior activists can and must do a lot to shape and guide the future. And remembering Ivan Ilyich on his death bed thinking he should have done more to help the poor, I intend to help my children and grandchildren however possible and work with my Congregational Church (UCC), which contributes to food banks, helps immigrants with housing and jobs, and supplies homeless people with food and warm clothing in the winter. I intend to mentor low-income and first-generation college students and candidates for elected office.

And of course, we seniors won't live forever, and as I contemplate passing on, I recall what Hunter S. Thompson once wrote: "Life is not a journey to the grave with the intention of arriving safely in a well-preserved body, but rather to skid in broadside, thoroughly used up, totally worn out, and loudly proclaiming, wow what a ride."

Thankfully there were important rides for American patriots like Nathan Hale who declared in 1776, "I regret that I have only one life to give for my country." Okay, yes, I have the same regret. I want to continue trying to fix things that are wrong in my country and in the world. And in 1880 political activist and abolitionist Harriet Tubman thundered, "If you are tired, keep going; if you are scared, keep going; if you are hungry, keep going; and if you want to taste freedom, keep going!"

I, for one, intend to keep going. I intend to grasp courage. I intend to fix things that are wrong but not by myself. How about you?

Feel free to email me at sue.schafer@comcast.

APPENDICES

Appendix A: Favorite Books

The 1619 Project (Nikole Hannah-Jones)
Against Our Will: Men, Women and Rape (Susan Brownmiller)
The Age of Innocence (Edith Wharton)
All Quiet on the Western Front (Erich Maria Remarque)
American Pastoral (Philip Roth)
The Audacity of Hope (Barack Obama)
Babbitt (Sinclair Lewis)
Bible
Bonfire of the Vanities (Tom Wolfe)
The Death of Ivan Ilyich (Leo Tolstoy)
The Diary of a Young Girl (Anne Frank)
Educated (Tara Westover)
Eleanor Roosevelt (Blanche Wiesen Cook)
Elmer Gantry (Sinclair Lewis)
Everyman (Philip Roth)
The Feminine Mystique (Betty Friedan)
Fierce Attachments: A Memoir (Vivian Gornick)
Fine Balance (Rohinton Mistry)
Gay Like Me: A Father Writes to His Son (Richie Jackson)
Gift from the Sea (Anne Morrow Lindberg)
The Good Earth (Pearl Buck)
The Grapes of Wrath (John Steinbeck)
House of the Spirits (Isabel Allende)
The Hypochondriac (Molière)
I and Thou (Martin Buber)
The Importance of Being Earnest (Oscar Wilde)

It Can't Happen Here (Sinclair Lewis)

It Takes a Village (Hillary Rodham Clinton)

Judy Garland: A Biography (Anne Edwards)

Madame Bovary (Gustave Flaubert)

Main Street (Sinclair Lewis)

Man's Search for Meaning (Viktor Frankl)

The Miser (Molière)

My Ántonia (Willa Cather)

Of Woman Born (Adrienne Rich)

Pavilion of Women (Pearl Buck)

The Power of Myth (Joseph Campbell)

The Quest for Certainty (John Dewey)

Second Sex (Simone de Beauvoir)

Secret of the Old Clock (Carolyn Keene from the Nancy Drew Mystery Stories)

Silent Spring (Rachel Carson)

Team of Rivals (Doris Kearns Goodwin)

Things Fall Apart (Chinua Achebe)

War and Peace (Leo Tolstoy)

When Bad Things Happen to Good People (Harold Kushner)

Zorba the Greek (Nikos Kazantzakis)

Appendix B: Favorite Quotations

If you know the source of who said or wrote these quotes, please email me at sue.schafer@comcast.net.

"A child is someone you carry in your body for nine months, in your arms for five years, and in your heart until the day you die."

"A chaque enfant qui naît, le monde recommence." (With every child who is born, the world begins again.)

"From everyone to whom much is given, much will be required, and from the one to whom much has been entrusted, even more will be demanded." (The Bible)

"You are always someone's teacher, the person to whom others look for inspiration." Ash Beckham

"Those who we love and lose are no longer where they were. They are now everywhere we are." St. John Chrysostom

"It's hard to be a woman. You must think like a man, act like a lady, look like a young girl, and work like a horse."

"Above all, be the hero of your life, not the victim." Nora Ephraim

"When your children are teenagers it's important to have a dog so that someone in your house is happy to see you." Nora Ephron

"It seems to me that the desire to get married is fundamental and primal in women. And it is followed almost immediately by an equally urgent desire to be single again." Nora Ephron

"I love people who harness themselves like an ox to a heavy cart—with massive patience, who strain in the mud to move things forward, and who do what has to be done again and again." Marge Piercy

"You are the hero of your own story." Maria Shriver

"Service is the rent we pay for being alive."

"When things don't work out for you, God has a better plan for you." Polly Hosack Haskell Pierce

"God is love." Mary Baker Eddy

"Divine love always has met and always will meet every human need." Mary Baker Eddy

"A mind is not a vessel to be filled but a fire to be kindled." Plutarch

"Every day is a blessing."

"I am living my dream."

"Tikkun Olam. [Hebrew] Repair the world, make the world more just, tolerant and equal through acts of charity, kindness and political action."

"Today is the tomorrow I dreamed about yesterday."

"Good morning! This is God. Today I will be handling all your problems. I won't be needing your help. Have a good day." God

"The more cunning a man is, the less he suspects that he will be caught in a simple thing." Dostoevsky

"Maybe I didn't live as I should have. But how could that be when I did everything as it was supposed to be done?" *The Death of Ivan Ilyich* by Leo Tolstoy

"He was a self-made man who owed his lack of success to nobody." Joseph Heller

"Follow your bliss and don't be afraid, and doors will open where you didn't know where they were going to be." Joseph Campbell

"Great minds discuss ideas, average minds discuss events, and small minds discuss people." Eleanor Roosevelt

"I have one life and one chance to make it count for something. My faith demands that I do whatever I can, wherever I am, for as long as I can, and with whatever I have to make a difference." President Jimmy Carter

"When you have a good idea and you think it's going to work, go ahead and do it. Because it is much easier to apologize than it is to get permission." Admiral Grace Hopper

"No good deed shall go unpunished." Thomas Aquinas

"He was good at nothing and he did it very well." *Elmer Gantry* by Sinclair Lewis

"He was born to be a senator. He never said anything important and he always said it sonorously." *Elmer Gantry* by Sinclair Lewis

"Deep in her soul she was waiting for something to happen." *Madame Bovary* by Gustave Flaubert

"Happy is the person who before dying has the good fortune to sail the Aegean Sea." *Zorba the Greek* by Nikos Kazantzakis

"When peace like a river upholds me each day, when sorrow like sea billows roll, whatever my lot, God has taught me to say, it is well, it is well with my soul." Phillip P. Bliss

"If you feel pain you are alive. If you feel other people's pain you are a human being." Leo Tolstoy

"Give me coffee for the things I can change and give me wine for the things I can't."

"I always wanted to be somebody, but I should have been more specific." Lily Tomlin

"Sometimes I worry about being a success in a mediocre world." Lily Tomlin

"Macho does not prove mucho." Zsa Zsa Gabor

"If I had learned to type I never would have made Brigadier General." Elizabeth P. Hoisington

"I'm not offended by all the dumb blond jokes because I know I'm not dumb and I also know that I am not blond." Dolly Parton

"Dog is a very small word for something that takes up so much room in your heart."

"You give but little when you give of your possessions. It is when you give of yourself that you truly give." Kahlil Gibran

"Your children are not your children. They are the sons and daughters of Life's longing for itself. They come through you but not from you, and though they are with you, yet they belong not to you." Kahlil Gibran

"Happiness is not a place to travel to. It's a way of getting there."

"Do not get lost in a sea of despair. Do not become bitter or hostile. Be hopeful, be optimistic. Never, ever be afraid to make some noise and get in good trouble, necessary trouble. We will find a way out of no way." Congressman John Lewis

"We never know how high we are, until we are called to rise. And then if we are true to plan, our statures touch the skies." Emily Dickinson

"I was there to hear your borning cry, I'll be there when you are old. I rejoiced the day you were baptized, and to see your life unfold." John Ylvisaker

"We shall overcome some day. Deep in my heart I do believe we shall overcome someday. We'll go hand in hand someday, we are not afraid, God will see us through, the truth will make us free, and we shall live in peace someday." C. A. Tindley

"Oh gentle presence, peace and joy and power; oh life divine that owns each waiting hour, God's love guards the nestling's faltering flight, so keep thou my child on upward wing tonight." Mary Baker Eddy

We turn not older with years, but newer every day. Emily Dickinson

Children and grand-children are the only form of immortality that we can be sure of. Peter Ustinov

Appendix C: Selected Honors

1970 Master of Arts in Psychology and Counseling, University of Colorado

1979 Doctor of Education Degree (Ed.D.), University of Northern Colorado

1982 Phi Delta Kappa Honorary, University of Northern Colorado

1985 Sportswomen of Colorado, Leadership Award

1986 National Association for Girls and Women in Sport, Coaches Council Award

1987 Order of the Kentucky Colonels, Women's Athletic Leadership Award

1991 Women's Sports Foundation, President's Award

1993 Denver Gates Tennis Center, Champion Award for Women Ranked 4.0

1993 Colorado Coaches of Girls Sports, Hall of Fame

1995 Colorado Congress of Foreign Language Teachers, Contribution Award

1996 Colorado Art Education Association Leadership Award

1997 Alliance for Colorado Theater, Leadership Award

1998 Colorado High School Activities Association, Service Award

2000 Denver Parents and Friends of Lesbians and Gays (PFLAG) Swan Leadership Award

2010 Jefferson County, Colorado Department of Health, Public Health Champion

2013 Colorado Developmental Disabilities Resource Center, Legislator of the Year Award

2012 Colorado Economic Development Council, Legislator of the Year Award

2010 Colorado House of Representatives, Mandatory Reporting of Elder Abuse, Prime House Sponsor

2012 Colorado House of Representatives, Gender-Fair Private Insurance Premiums, Prime House Sponsor

2013 Colorado House of Representatives, Civil Unions Law, Prime House Sponsor

2014 Colorado House of Representatives, March of Dimes Champion Award

2014 Colorado Council on Aging, Champion for Services Award

Appendix D: Other Publications by Susan P. Schafer

1979 <u>A Description of an Inservice Workshop for Raising Teachers' Awareness of Sex Discrimination in Education,</u> University of Northern Colorado

1984 <u>Sports Need You: A Working Model for the Equity Professional: How to Increase the Number of Women and Minorities in Athletic Coaching, Officiating, Administration and Governance,</u> Colorado Department of Education

2015 <u>Colorado House District 24 Leadership: Turning Red to Blue in Thirty Years,</u> Jefferson County, Colorado Democratic Party

ACKNOWLEDGMENTS

Debby Bernau

Carly Catt

Sandy Chapman

David Conner

Lakewood Public Library, Lakewood, Colorado

Launch Team Volunteers

Mikyle Lockwood

Gaye Lowe-Kaplan

Janice McDermott

Barbara L. Nash

Judith G. Nelson

Carole A. Oglesby

Mary Tate-Phillips

Claudia Schmitt

Christine Shelton

Jan Silverstein

Bonnie Taher

Constance Wise

Made in United States
Troutdale, OR
06/22/2024

20739405R00163